Just One Verse

The Book of Mormon
Mosiah 25:10

Denalee Call Chapman

DEDICATION

For my father,
Dennis Boyd Call.
"The more I think about it, the more I learn."
You told me that one day when we
were talking about one of your
favorite scriptures.
Thank you for teaching me to ponder
and
to "seek learning, even by study and also by faith."
(Doctrine & Covenants 88:118)

BOOK COVER ARTWORK BY
Ken Turner
None Could Deliver Them
TurnerChapmanGallery.com

CONTENTS

And again, when they thought of the immediate goodness of God, and his power in delivering Alma and his brethren out of the hands of the Lamanites and of bondage, they did raise their voices and give thanks to God.

The Book of Mormon, Mosiah 25:10

FOREWORD

Alma held a high position in the kingdom. He was one of many of the priests of King Noah[1] – a very wicked man. King Noah was gluttonous and greedy and cruel. A prophet by the name of Abinadi came into the land to preach repentance.[2] He exposed the king and all those who were perverting the ways of the Lord. The people became angry with Abinadi. He was taken before the king and his priests in a court-like setting. Abinadi spoke boldly and continued to testify against the people even though his life was threatened by the king. Of course, this made the king and the other wicked people angry. But there was one, Alma, who believed[3] the words of Abinadi. He pled with the king to release the prophet, but instead of softening his heart, King Noah threw Alma out, then sent his people to kill him. Alma escaped those who were pursuing him and hid for several days – long enough to write Abinadi's words.[4] I imagine this was a time of great soul-searching for Alma. We know that during this time and shortly thereafter Alma "repented of his sins and iniquities."[5] And then he acted some more on his recent conversion. Alma went among the people privately, preaching the same words that Abinadi had taught. Those who believed on Alma's words gathered together in a beautiful secluded area – away from the notice of the king. It was here that they were edified together as they heard God's word preached by Alma. The people were overjoyed when they learned that through baptism they could be given greater access to the Spirit. In fact, "they clapped their hands for joy, and

---

[1] The Book of Mormon, Mosiah 11

[2] The Book of Mormon, Mosiah 11-17

[3] The Book of Mormon, Mosiah 17:2

[4] The Book of Mormon, Mosiah 17:4

[5] The Book of Mormon, Mosiah 18:1

exclaimed: This is the desire of our hearts."[6] The very day that Alma taught the importance of baptism, over two hundred people were baptized.   The number of believers grew steadily and quickly. In fact, there was so much success in bringing individuals to Christ that the king took notice. He "discovered a movement among the people"[7] and sent soldiers to kill the group. When Alma's people learned that they were no longer safe, they gathered their families and their belongings and fled.[8] By this time there were about four hundred and fifty converts. It must have been quite an exodus, hundreds of people with their food, animals and tents. These good people were strengthened by the Lord and protected from King Noah's army. They traveled for eight days and settled in another beautiful place. Here, they grew together through hard work, love, righteousness and obedience. They were so unified that they shared freely with each other, both physically and spiritually, so all were taken care of. This was done not by mandate, but by desire.[9]

Understanding how happy and peaceful Alma's people were, and also understanding how hard they were working to keep their baptismal covenants, it's heartbreaking to know what came next: while they were working in the fields one day, a Lamanite army came to attack. As the army was drawing nearer, the people gathered and Alma spoke to them. He reminded them how they had been delivered in the past and that the Lord is aware of them. And then they all prayed. They prayed for safety and protection, and they prayed that the Lord would soften the hearts of the Lamanites. I'm certain that Alma and the other leaders also prayed for inspiration and direction. "And it came to pass that the

---

[6] The Book of Mormon, Mosiah 18:11

[7] The Book of Mormon, Mosiah 18:32

[8] The Book of Mormon, Mosiah 23:1

[9] The Book of Mormon, Mosiah 23

Lord did soften the hearts of the Lamanites. And Alma and his brethren went forth and delivered themselves up into their hands."[10]

The Lamanites were cunning, but a Nephite dissenter was even more cunning. Amulon had gained favor with the king of the Lamanites and was given authority over the people of Alma. He set taskmasters over Alma's people who abused and ruled over them.[11]   Amulon was especially dastardly.   He was a contemporary of Alma, having known him when they were both priests in King Noah's court. So Amulon used every ounce of authority granted him by the Lamanite king. Not only did he require physical obedience, but he also commanded Alma's people that they must not pray. In fact, he set guards over the people with instructions to kill any who prayed.[12]   These righteous, peaceful people stopped praying aloud, but continued to pray in their hearts. Their faith was strong, and they knew that God would hear their thoughts. Alma's people were visited with peace and promised by the Lord that "…I will … ease the burdens which are put upon your shoulders, that even you cannot feel them upon your backs, even while you are in bondage; and this will I do that ye may stand as witnesses for me hereafter, and that ye may know of a surety that I, the Lord God, do visit my people in their afflictions."[13] This promise was fulfilled. The people were strengthened. They remained in bondage to Amulon and the Lamanites, and continued to be burdened with physical labor and abuse, yet "they could bear up their burdens with ease …"[14] Eventually, Alma and his people miraculously escaped. We don't

---

[10] The Book of Mormon, Mosiah 23:29

[11] The Book of Mormon, Mosiah 24:1

[12] The Book of Mormon, Mosiah 24:11

[13] The Book of Mormon, Mosiah 24:14

[14] The Book of Mormon, Mosiah 24:15

know how long their bondage lasted, but we do know that they "did submit cheerfully and with patience to all the will of the Lord"[15] while they were still in bondage. The escape took place following a night of preparation. With the Lord's help, Alma's entire group was able to leave while all the guards and taskmasters were sleeping.

After a full day and night of travel the people rested and pitched their tents. Their first order of business was to offer prayers of gratitude for their deliverance.[16] Their rest was short-lived, though. The Lamanites were in pursuit of them so they packed up and continued their escape. After twelve days on the go, Alma and his people arrived in the land of Zarahemla where righteous King Mosiah and his people "did ... receive them with joy."[17]

King Mosiah called for a gathering of all citizens. Among other things, this meeting consisted of a reading of the record of Alma and his people, including their being placed in bondage and their escape. "And now, when Mosiah had made an end of reading the records, his people who tarried in the land were struck with wonder and amazement. For they knew not what to think; for when they beheld those that had been delivered out of bondage they were filled with exceedingly great joy. And again, when they thought of their brethren who had been slain by the Lamanites they were filled with sorrow, and even shed many tears of sorrow. *And again, when they thought of the immediate goodness of God, and his power in delivering Alma and his brethren out of the hands of the Lamanites and of bondage, they did raise their voices and give thanks to God.*"[18]

---

[15] The Book of Mormon, Mosiah 24:15

[16] The Book of Mormon, Mosiah 24:21-22

[17] The Book of Mormon 24:25

[18] The Book of Mormon 25:7-10 (italics added)

PREFACE

I was sitting on an airplane contemplating the past ten days. I didn't know until the afternoon before that I would be leaving early that morning. I closed my eyes and began to pray once again. During my prayer of thanks, a section of scripture came to mind. I prayed, *I'm so grateful for the "immediate goodness of God."*[19] It seemed the perfect phrase to describe my feelings. I spent much of the airplane ride examining the verse of scripture that captured this phrase.

It was during a visit with my parents a couple of years earlier that I learned the value of immersing myself in *just one verse.* It's been amazing to me how much one can continue to learn from parents through the years. Each time I'm blessed to visit with my parents, my faith grows and I glean spiritual value from my time with them.

I remember sitting around the dinner table as a teenager, all of us being encouraged by both parents to share our thoughts on everything from our day's experiences to politics to gospel doctrine. Although it was those early years that taught me to examine scripture for myself, that desire to learn and personally apply scripture has grown as I've participated in gospel discussions with them over the past few years. Whether it's preparation for one of their upcoming lessons, or re-reading a General Conference talk for Family Home Evening, my greatest growth comes as we discuss some of the words we've read. It's the discussion of God's word that promotes the increase of testimony within

---

19 The Book of Mormon, Mosiah 25:10

me – increased faith and knowledge that comes straight from the Holy Ghost. Oh, how I've appreciated my parents teaching me, even now, to cherish the Lord's word and to "make [it] mine."[20]

It is my testimony that there is great value to be found in every verse - indeed, in every word, included in the scriptures. As we fill our minds with scriptures, focusing on what application there is for us, our spiritual growth increases and our daily lives improve. In fact, among other things, we're promised that as we "let virtue garnish [our] thoughts unceasingly,"[21] we will have the Holy Ghost with us constantly. He will be our companion! What a wonderful blessing. Additionally, we're promised that "doctrines [will] distill upon [our] soul[s]."[22] This means to me that I will be able to understand, not only in my mind and heart, but with my *whole being,* things that can only be comprehended through the Spirit. I was talking with my daughter recently about scripture study. Somehow personal righteousness and worthiness seeped into the conversation. As we talked, I stated a truth that I only recognized as the words came out of my mouth: Satan will attack us in sneaky ways. One of those ways is to make us question ourselves, our personal standing before God, our worthiness. I realized, and stated at that time, that when I am truly immersed in treasuring the word of the Lord, there is no room for Satan to tempt me to focus on myself. When I'm really studying - that is, reading, pondering and praying about His word - I'm happy. *And I am confident* in regards to my standing before God. Another blessing promised as we fill our minds with virtue is that our

---

[20] Doctrinal New Testament Commentary 1-662, Bruce R. McConkie

[21] Doctrine and Covenants 121:45

[22] Doctrine and Covenants 121:45

"confidence [will] wax strong in the presence of God."[23] Truly, treasuring the scriptures completely and regularly will fill us with virtue and give us the confidence spoken of.

However we choose to make the scriptures a part of our lives, it is worth the time and effort invested. Feasting daily on the scriptures has meant something different to me at various stages of my life. Right now, I benefit greatly from studying *Just One Verse*.

---

23 Doctrine and Covenants 121:45

CHAPTER 1
AND AGAIN

Taken in context, these two words *and again* are a reminder of the lengthy pondering and praying that the people of Zarahemla were involved in. King Mosiah had just read the records of the people of Alma to his kingdom. "And now, when Mosiah had made an end of reading the records, his people who tarried in the land were struck with wonder and amazement. For they knew not what to think; for when they beheld those that had been delivered out of bondage they were filled with exceedingly great joy. *And again,* when they thought of their brethren who had been slain by the Lamanites they were filled with sorrow, and even shed many tears of sorrow. *And again ...*"[24] To have so many feelings, there had to be some real considering, pondering and even introspection.

On a recent airplane ride I sat next to a woman and her eight-year-old daughter. They were clearly excited about their trip and it was enjoyable to watch their interaction. Shortly before takeoff the two started talking in a foreign language. That surprised me, because I hadn't caught hint of an accent when they were

---

[24] The Book of Mormon, Mosiah 25:7-10 (italics added)

speaking in English. This intrigued me and so I started a conversation with the two which lasted the entire flight. I found that the family is from Poland. Mother and daughter were traveling to a figure skating competition – the daughter's first. It was exciting for them because on the same day the daughter would be competing on the ice, her brother was in a ski competition in a neighboring state – their father accompanying him. I learned much about this remarkable family and was especially interested at the mother (Ania) using the phrase *and again* a couple of dozen times. As she spoke, each time she used the phrase, *and again*, I realized she was voicing one more statement to support a general point she was making. In Ania's case, each thought that began with *and again* spoke to the importance she and her husband placed on growing a strong, loving family. From supporting their children's sports ambitions, to transitioning jobs so she can be at home when the children are home, to giving the kids a strong sense of their heritage, all these parents do is in support of family solidarity. *And again* emphasized that truth.

So, could it be that the prophet Mormon, abridging this record of Mosiah's people, hoped to emphasize something? I think so. *And again* in these verses tells me that:

> 1. Mosiah and his people were good to the core. They acted out of love, rather than duty. Imagine hundreds of people – refugees, really – arriving. Mosiah didn't just allow entrance into his land; he made sure that his people knew who had arrived and what their circumstances were. This good community not only opened their land to Alma's people, but they opened their hearts as well. They were so touched by the experiences Alma's people had endured, that they went beyond sharing their land ... they offered strong prayers of gratitude for Alma's people's deliverance. I can imagine what is not recorded in the

scriptures: things such as feeding the new community members; helping build homes; dividing and gifting land; organizing social functions.

2. The people of Mosiah had been taught about prayer and service. It was a natural action for the people of Zarahemla to pray in all sincerity. But beyond that, their prayers were accompanied by action – they welcomed Alma's people. Mosiah's people knew the truth that was later taught by Amulek during his sermon about prayer: "And now behold, my beloved brethren, I say unto you, do not suppose that this is all; for after ye have done all these things, if ye turn away the needy, and the naked, and visit not the sick and afflicted, and impart of your substance, if ye have, to those who stand in need – I say unto you, if ye do not any of these things, behold, your prayer is vain, and availeth you nothing, and ye are as hypocrites who do deny the faith."[25] They prayed, yes. But they also acted. It was Mosiah's father, King Benjamin, who worked alongside his people and whose words about service are vital to remember: "And behold, I tell you these things that ye may learn wisdom; that ye may learn that when ye are in the service of your fellow beings ye are only in the service of your God."[26]

3. King Mosiah led by example in teaching his people to continue on a righteous course. Just as his father had done before him, Mosiah expected no more from his people than he, himself, was willing to do. The very fact that he gathered his people so they could be given the same information about the new community members

---

[25] The Book of Mormon, Alma 34:28

[26] The Book of Mormon, Mosiah 2:17

that he was given, is exemplary. There were no barking orders to open their borders without explanation. Rather, his people trusted him – opened their land first and welcomed Alma's people in - *then quickly* their trust in their king was confirmed as he brought them into his circle and shared all that he knew. I imagine that King Mosiah walked among his people on a daily basis. Instead of isolating himself in luxury and making demands of his people, he taught them to respect every individual – because that is what he did.

4. These people were humble and recognized the Lord's hand in others' lives as well as their own. The fact that they willingly gathered to hear about what was going on in others' lives, were heartbroken at their losses, experienced pure joy at their recently granted freedom, and attributed the miraculous circumstances to God, are proof of their humility. It is humility that encourages reliance on Heavenly Father and helps one to recognize His hand in our lives. It is humility that allows sincere, heartfelt prayer. It is humility that helps us to be grateful.

5. The people of Mosiah were empathetic beyond what many of us can imagine. Gathered together immediately after arrival of the refugees, the people of Zarahemla needed only to hear about the hardships that the refugees had endured in order to feel their pain and their joy. They felt it so strongly that they cried and they prayed and they expressed joy and relief. This is before they even got to know the individuals! These are people who really understood that we are all brothers and sisters, and that all of us are affected by one another.

6. Likely, these people understood the concept of praying without ceasing. This thought is supported by

reading that their first reaction, upon hearing what their new friends had been through, was to pray. It wasn't the king who said, "Ok, let's all offer a prayer of thanks now." The people, themselves, were so overcome with emotion that they immediately raised their voices in prayer.

Mormon, in abridging this experience, emphasized to us (because the Book of Mormon was written for our day)[27] the goodness of King Mosiah and his people when he used the phrase *and again.* Perhaps this was emphasized so we might use them as an example of the type of people we are striving to become. These were not extraordinary people – not movie stars or sports heroes. They were ordinary citizens. But they were people who humbly knew their divinity and recognized divinity in others.

In Noah Webster's 1828 American Dictionary of the English Language, the word *again* is described this way: "All the uses of this word carry in them the ideas of return or repetition." Repetition is an important part of learning. As we consider how a child learns to walk, we realize that it is through repetition (just as anything a child learns to do) that success is finally achieved. And here's the clincher – the child keeps trying, over and over again, as we encourage him. When he falls we don't berate him. In fact, we think it's kind of cute! For some children it takes months of practicing before walking is mastered. And during those months we all cheer and encourage through every attempt. The child learns that falling isn't failure – but rather, it is practice. And the child repeats over and over and over again the same process, until at last, he is walking. Repetition doesn't mean something is too hard for us; it doesn't mean we're not smart; and it isn't boring. Repetition is a means to accomplishment. It is through repetition

---

[27] LDS General Conference, April, 1975, The Book of Mormon is the Word of God, Ezra Taft Benson

that we will eventually become exalted. It is through repetition that growth takes place.

Several years ago we lived in a two-story home, with the kitchen on the upper floor. The climate was such that we kept the kitchen window open most of the year. It was one of those windows that opened toward the outside by cranking it on the inside. One year we were surprised and excited to see that a pair of robins was building their nest right on the ledge of that opened window. It was early in the spring when we first took notice of the two birds as they diligently flew back and forth. One would come with a beak filled with twigs, followed shortly by the other with some grass and weeds. This happened over and over again, hour after hour. For days the two robins repeated their efforts. Sometimes they would be gone for several minutes before returning with mud or twigs, but always they would show up with a completely full beak. It looked like hard work! They seemed to not tire at all as they continued to fly away and then return again and again. Eventually their repetitive movements were over. At least for a while. The nest was completed and apparently met their expectations because within a couple of days we noticed that the momma bird was sitting in the nest, rarely leaving. Repetition was required for our beautiful robins to progress as they were made to do. It was awe-inspiring to watch the dedication of both of them through their nest-building and beyond. They were fixed on a purpose and nothing would stop their progress. Interestingly, through it all – the monotonous back and forth, the searching for appropriate material, the heavy carrying of excessive nest fodder on each trip – the birds sang. We came to recognize when our birds were near, when they were working, and when they were playing. They had different songs – but every song was beautiful. Sometimes as the birds were building their nest, and then later as they were caring for their young, we would sit quietly in the kitchen or we'd be outside and just watch for a good amount of time. It was intriguing and incredibly relaxing to watch our robins at work. But it wasn't just watching that captivated us – it was listening. We learned a lot of lessons that spring. One of those lessons was that repetition is a good thing, and that there is joy to be found even in the mundane repetition of work. *And again* is a phrase that reminds us to keep practicing. It is repetition that creates progression and leads us to our eventual goals.

Repetition leads us to another possible meaning for *and again*. The word "remember" is used 321 times in the scriptures. From The Old Testament's "*Remember* the Sabbath day, to keep it holy,"[28] to the angels at the empty tomb telling the women, "He is not here, but is risen: *remember* how he spake unto you when he was yet in Galilee,"[29] to the Book of Mormon prophet Helaman's advice to his sons: "… *remember, remember* that it is upon the rock of our Redeemer, who is Christ, the Son of God, that ye must build your foundation,"[30] to a reminder from the Lord in this last dispensation, "*Remember* the worth of souls is great in the sight of God,"[31] we are reminded *repeatedly* of the importance of *remembering*. Why do we create To Do Lists? So we will *remember* what we want to accomplish. Why do we write our goals and put them in conspicuous places throughout our home? So we will *remember* what we're striving to do. Why do we read the same books of scripture repeatedly throughout our lives? So we will *remember* what the Lord wants us to know.

Over the past couple of years I've been traveling a lot to spend time as a helper in my parents' home as they work through the

---

[28] The Old Testament, Exodus 20:8 (italics added)

[29] The New Testament, Luke 24:6 (italics added)

[30] The Book of Mormon, Helaman 5:12 (italics added)

[31] The Doctrine & Covenants 18:10 (italics added)

normal struggles of aging. My husband and I were talking recently about my upcoming trip and more than once we used the word *again*. We talked about the positive effect of traveling *again and again* to my parents' home. Interestingly, there wasn't talk about the positive effect for my parents – it was all the good things that were coming to *us* because of visiting *again* with my parents. I am so grateful for the unforeseen bits of wisdom I've gained, little miracles I've witnessed, joyful moments I've participated in, and testimony growth I've received through these visits that have taken place *again and again.* What a positive bit of surprise blessings I've been gifted! And what a wonderful reminder that the Lord offers us joyful opportunities as we grasp onto the concept of *and again.* Whether we focus on those two little words reminding us to *remember*, or to find joy in *repetition,* or to discover what the Lord is *emphasizing* to us, *and again* is a phrase certainly worth pondering!

CHAPTER 2
WHEN THEY THOUGHT

Isn't it such a gift that we are able to think for ourselves? Thinking is a many-layered action. It can be as simple as a single thought popping into our heads, then being dismissed; or it can be that same thought taking root as we ponder, consider, explore and eventually act. All actions are preceded by a thought. So when we consider this phrase, *when they thought*, there is much to explore.

My angel mother passed away recently. I miss her, but I also feel her near often. I talk to Mom every day and hope that she's able to break away and be with me to hear what I'm telling her. One beautiful autumn day I was riding my bike. There was a slight breeze and the air was crisp and comfortable. As I rode under some colorful trees and the leaves danced down from their branches, I was in awe of autumn. I took a deep, calming breath that really ended up being more invigorating than calming. I started talking out loud to Mom. "Mother, look at this! And the smell!!! It smells so clean and fresh and perfect. Don't you love it?" And then I wondered – *When our spirits are separated from our bodies, the time between death and resurrection, do we have all five senses? Can Mom smell right now? Maybe spirits, yet to be reunited with their bodies, actually have access to the five senses I know about and then some ...* I thought on it for a while

21

then went on to other things. A few days later I was talking with my sister over the phone. I asked what she thought about that. Her answer was no better than mine except that she added something like, "It's thinking like that, that leads to revelation." She then went on to talk about Joseph Smith, the young prophet, knowing he needed baptism, but also knowing he should not join any of the churches. How, then could he be baptized? It was that active thinking – pondering, really – that led to the eventual restoration of the Priesthood.[32]

It was the prophet, Joseph F. Smith, whose active pondering led to the 138th section of the Doctrine and Covenants[33] - a section which teaches comforting and instructional truths about the Spirit World. Interestingly, his pondering included reflection.[34] He also wondered.[35] How often do we allow our thinking to go so far to include *reflection* and *wonder*? This validates the suggestion that we all need quiet time. Whether the season of our lives allows for daily time alone, or just a few minutes in a week, we really need it. We need time to consciously think. I believe our sleep allows for active thinking, but we often don't remember where our thinking led us when we awaken. If we're at a stage in our lives where we're required to focus on little children, never really being able to carve out significant alone time, we may have to settle for the bits and pieces of uninterrupted sleep to really get some thinking done. If that's the case, keeping a notebook and pen by the bed is helpful in remembering what we've learned through our nocturnal thinking. Unless, of course, you're like me and can't read your writing in the morning. ☺ Latter-day prophets have instructed us to record the thoughts that come to us as we

---

[32] Joseph Smith History 1:68-70

[33] Doctrine and Covenants, Section 138

[34] Doctrine and Covenants, 138:2

[35] Doctrine and Covenants, 138:28,29

ponder - even those thoughts that come to us as we are actively thinking in our sleep. Elder Richard G. Scott shared his experience of increased knowledge as he pondered, received instruction, wrote down that instruction, and then pondered and prayed over it some more.[36] President Henry B. Eyring also taught the importance of writing, or recording, messages from Heaven.[37] His was in reference to recognizing God's hand in our lives. President Eyring talked of focusing our minds on the goodness of God and then being sure to preserve those thoughts - for ourselves to consider at a needed time, and for our posterity to be blessed with a glimpse into our lives and our thoughts.

Our thoughts are valuable, not only to us, but as President Eyring taught, to our children and future generations as well. I've known something of that gift as I've read over the few writings of my ancestors. But I've been strongly impacted by reading my mother's thoughts. She was diligent in writing. I've been studying recently, from one of my mother's sets of scriptures. My study is slow-going, as there is so much more to read! Besides highlighting and underlining, my mother wrote carefully in the margins, above and beneath select verses, and on sticky notes when there wasn't room on the actual page. I have no doubt as to the strength of my mother's testimony! But it's not just knowing *what* she knew that is a blessing to me. Her thoughts, recorded on paper, have sparked thoughts of my own. They have given me little seeds, that, through pondering, continued study, and prayer, have led to some much desired inspiration and direction from Heavenly Father. Oh how grateful I am that my mother not only pondered, but also wrote!

---

36 LDS General Conference, October 2009, To Acquire Spiritual Guidance, Richard G. Scott

37 LDS General Conference, October 2007, O Remember, Remember, Henry B. Eyring

It wasn't until the Book of Mormon prophet Nephi, pondered upon the truths his father taught[38] the family, that he had his own spiritual confirmation and tutoring. Interestingly, and importantly, Nephi's pondering was preceded by *desire* and belief - including *faith* in the Lord.[39] And so I ask myself: *What does my thinking consist of? Is it a haphazard scattering of thoughts, or are my thoughts intentional? Do I have a true desire to have my thoughts be productive? And do I really believe that my thoughts will lead to the direction and instruction I need?* I'm sure that when Lehi taught his family about what he learned about the Plan of Happiness from his dream, that everyone was intrigued. I'm sure it sparked interest, and maybe even desire in all of them. But what then? Some of the family members did not turn to the Lord for understanding. In fact, they began a contentious debate.[40] Sure, they *thought* about Lehi's words. But it wasn't preceded by desire and belief. Their thinking was fueled by selfishness, murmuring, pride, and a complete lack of faith. Pride is demonstrated when we close our minds, projecting the feeling that no understanding can be better than my own on this subject. This can be applied to General Conference talks, too. Am I willing to open not only my mind, but also my heart to change that I need to make in my own life? So, when I hear things, or read things, or consider things that are difficult to understand - where do I go from there? To be productive pondering, it must be guided by the Spirit. Even thoughts that are not huge revelations or monumental discoveries - little thoughts that are seemingly unimportant - without the Spirit they cannot develop into productive thoughts. That's not to say that we can't achieve anything without the Spirit guiding us. There are many in the world who have proven otherwise. But when we look at the

---

38 The Book of Mormon, 1 Nephi 8

39 The Book of Mormon, 1 Nephi 11:1, 3, 4

40 The Book of Mormon, 1 Nephi 15:2

eternal picture, and realize that mortality truly is a time "to prepare to meet God,"[41] wouldn't we want all of our thoughts to lead us closer to exaltation rather than keeping us stagnant or moving further away?

Way back in 1973, Elder Boyd K. Packer talked to the youth about thoughts. The imagery he used is great: "The mind is like a stage. Except when we are asleep the curtain is always up. There is always some act being performed on that stage. It may be a comedy, a tragedy, interesting or dull, good or bad; but always there is some act playing on the stage of the mind. Have you noticed that without any real intent on your part, in the middle of almost any performance, a shady little thought may creep in from the wings and attract your attention? These delinquent thoughts will try to upstage everybody. If you permit them to go on, all thoughts of any virtue will leave the stage. You will be left, because you consented to it, to the influence of unrighteous thoughts. If you yield to them, they will enact for you on the stage of your mind anything to the limits of your toleration. They may enact a theme of bitterness, jealousy, or hatred. It may be vulgar, immoral, even depraved. When they have the stage, if you let them, they will devise the most clever persuasions to hold your attention. They can make it interesting all right, even convince you that it is innocent—for they are but thoughts. What do you do at a time like that, when the stage of your mind is commandeered by the imps of unclean thinking?—whether they be the gray ones that seem almost clean or the filthy ones which leave no room for doubt."[42] And then he gives the key to keeping those ugly and unproductive thoughts off of the stage of our minds. "Once you learn to clear the stage of your mind from unworthy thoughts, keep it busy with learning worthwhile things. Change your environment so that you have things about you that

---

41 The Book of Mormon, Alma 34:32

42 LDS General Conference, October 1973, Inspiring Music -Worthy Thoughts, Boyd K. Packer

will inspire good and uplifting thoughts." So, until the desire and belief are strong enough to master all the thoughts that pop into our heads, following Elder Packer's advice to change our environment is a great starting point. The importance of watching our thoughts was emphasized anciently by King Benjamin during his last address to his people. Near the end of his very tender sermon, King Benjamin emphasized the need to remember and explained that because he couldn't specify every sin to avoid, we must all check ourselves. In his words, "...watch yourselves, and *your thoughts*, and your words, and your deeds ..."[43]

James Allen, the author of *As a Man Thinketh*, in the foreword of his little book tells us: "[The book's] object being to stimulate men and women to the discovery and perception of the truth that 'They themselves are makers of themselves' by virtue of the thoughts which they choose and encourage..." This thought, in concert with Elder Packer's advice, gives great encouragement to controlling what we allow on the stage of our minds. When we consider what we hope to become, where we hope to be, and what we hope to achieve, we realize that it all begins with our thoughts. How important it is to work on controlling our thoughts! And when we realize the great gift that thinking is, we can't help but also feel a *responsibility* to control our thoughts. Thinking is all about agency. We are all, each of us, free to choose how we think. Not only as a gift from God, but it's actually impossible for *anyone* to take away that freedom. The rest of our freedoms can be taken from us by unrighteous, unkind, or violent people. But not how we choose to think. Many Holocaust survivors are proof of that truth. Think of Corrie Ten Boom and her sister, Betsy. They not only worked in the resistance movement, providing food and shelter for those seeking refuge from the Nazis, but they also provided the healing balm of God's

---

43 The Book of Mormon, Mosiah 4:30 (Italics added)

love. With a Bible that they snuck into the work camp they were sent to, the sisters held worship services. Betsy's dying words to Corrie were these: "There is no pit so deep that He is not deeper still."[44] Certainly, Betsy was in control of her thoughts. Through their gifted way of thinking, Betsy and Corrie brought peace to many people - even years after the war was over. They even brought peace to those who were their enemies. All of this because of choosing to think in productive, positive ways.

We are, each of us, more in control of our thoughts than we may currently believe. Phrases such as, "They make me so angry!" and "I can't help it - it's just the way I think" are destructive in that they emphasize the lie that we are not in control of our own thoughts. That is a lie that Satan thrives on. We may *choose* to give our minds to Satan so he can control what we think about. But it is our choice! Do we dwell on things that we wish were not in our minds? It's our responsibility and *our gift* to choose otherwise. It may take practice, and in fact, probably will! Like any habit, we can train our minds to think about specific things. We can kick Satan right out of our heads and fill our thoughts with light. But we must be ready, as soon as we *choose* to take control of our thoughts, with specific thoughts to replace those that we kick out. Otherwise, we leave an empty space that serves as an invitation to Satan to come fill it again. As we determine what kinds of thoughts we want in our heads, and then practice putting them there, it will get easier and easier to have control of our minds. By doing so, we are reclaiming our agency and weakening Satan's hold on us.

Thinking is work! Anyone ever get a headache from thinking so hard? I have. Sometimes I just want a break from thinking - and I sometimes hope that's what sleep will bring. But then I awake the next morning only to realize that I've done most of my

---

44 The Hiding Place

thinking work in my sleep ... problems solved! So perhaps my *conscious* thinking just hasn't been done in the right way. Maybe, if I analyze how I am able to work things out in my thoughts during the night, I might be more productive in my think-work during the day. So what do I know about my nighttime dream-thinking? Well, it's usually creative. Often I figure things out, not because I've created a list in my sleep, but rather because everything has played out in my mind. Usually in an entertaining way.   And so, what part does imagination play in productive thinking? Well, for one thing, we know that all things are created spiritually before they are created temporally.[45] That's well and good when we're talking about our spirits being created before our bodies were; and when we're talking about the creation of the Earth.   But doesn't it still apply when we're talking about creating situations in our lives? Not just situations and intangible things - but even when we're creating physical things. Don't our projects end better when we've planned in our minds how it will come to be, start to finish? What person builds a house without a blueprint? What Olympian takes the gold without playing the event over and over in his mind? If that's the case (and it is) then why should we expect to create or accomplish *anything* without first thinking it through? How can we possibly expect great things to happen without planning them and executing them in our minds? And how can we expect and hope for good things if we fill our thoughts with negativity and sour outcomes? Truly, thinking in a productive way is very hard work. It takes concentration, discipline, dedication of time, and a lot of energy.

But what about things that we don't have direct control over? What role does *thinking* play in the requests we make of Heavenly Father? While waiting on the Lord, doesn't thinking constitute active pursuit? Because our prayers are often answered with

---

45 The Pearl of Great Price, Moses 3:5

thoughts, doesn't it make sense that we need to intentionally and consistently *think,* so that in the Lord's time we will recognize the answers we're seeking as they come into our minds as thoughts? I don't expect that the Lord will force a thought - an answer to our prayers - into our minds which are not already working hard in the thinking area. That's not to say that we should always have our minds busy. Sometimes clearing our minds and creating a blank slate, will allow the whisperings of the Spirit to enter. This is also active work. And I do expect that as we participate in all the aspects of active thinking (pondering, wondering, exploring, reflecting, seeking, clearing) eventually the answers we are requesting will appear and we will recognize them for the truths that they are. Interestingly, my experience is that when I am actively engaged in seeking truth through the ways we've been taught - that is, scripture study, prayer, worship, pondering - then I am blessed with answers, often unrelated to what I'm studying or thinking about at that moment. Let me share some personal examples of this:

Several years ago we moved from one state to another. We purchased a home in our new state before selling our old house and so, for a time we had two mortgage payments. Our timing was really bad, as the recession hit shortly after our move. We paid top dollar for our new home, and were having a hard time selling our old. We prayed over it, talked about options, and took every action we felt inspired to do. Still, month after month the house stayed on the market. One day, while sitting in Sacrament Meeting and honestly listening to the speaker, an unrelated thought popped into my mind. I remembered a recent General Conference address and knew that as soon as possible I should reread it. When we got home, I pulled it out and read it. The conference talk referenced payment of tithes and offerings and the promised blessings associated. I felt the clear prompting that we could, and should, call down the earned blessings of heaven as we prayed again for our house to sell. That night, my husband and I prayed in earnest, this time with the confidence that we had previously been lacking. The next day, Monday, we accepted an offer on our house. I learned many lessons from that experience. One of them was the truth that consistent, faith-filled thinking prepared my mind for the revelation we needed to bring about the blessing Heavenly Father was already prepared to give to us.

I recently opened up one of my journals to see a single statement: *Maybe we need to rethink our methods in respect to [our child's] schooling.* My husband and I talked for months - maybe even years - about how tense things were in our home when we would discuss school work with one of our children. It was taking a toll on all of us, but especially on the relationship I had with this child. We both gave it a lot of thought and made it a matter of prayer. But the answer didn't come immediately. I remember one day while doing housework the answer popped into my head. I couldn't believe how simple it was! Ingenious, actually! I also couldn't believe I hadn't thought of it before. But here it was - the answer we had been seeking. Much, much thought went into this problem before the simple, divine answer came. And it was definitely inspired, because it changed everything. I marveled that the answer came while doing housework - not while reading my scriptures or doing some other "spiritual" thing. But that doesn't mean that I didn't read scriptures seeking the answer - I did! Often! I know from my experiences that answers come *in the Lord's time* when we are putting forth the appropriate effort. And almost always, that work includes thinking.

There are other things - truths, actually - that I can't quite grasp. I read them or hear them; then my mind understands the concept and I accept that they are truths; but I can't grab ahold of them and make them mine. As ambiguous as this sounds, I think it's something we can all relate to. For example, I grew up being taught, and believing, that we are all children of our Heavenly

Father. We are all divine. We are brothers and sisters. But it wasn't until I was 21 years old and a new missionary that I was able to catch that truth and make it mine. In other words, I finally understood it through pure intelligence flowing into me[46] - or in other words, I was taught by the Holy Ghost. This happened on one of my first proselyting days. I served in Japan and rather than knocking on doors, we went to the crowded train stations and would stop people as they were coming and going, introduce ourselves and invite them to hear about God. The Japanese I learned in the Missionary Training Center didn't get me very far those first few days. No one could understand me, and I certainly couldn't understand them. My companion and I walked to the train station, and then she showed me where to stand and told me that she would be only a few yards away - within sight - and we would talk to people individually. I was afraid. I didn't want to do it. Everyone looked scary and foreign to me and I was truly frightened. I was near a tall pole, so I backed up against it and closed my eyes. I prayed, "Please, Heavenly Father. Please help me. I am afraid." When I opened my eyes and looked at the hordes of Japanese people hustling toward or away from the trains, I saw something different than what it looked like just a minute earlier. Absolutely pure intelligence flowed to my very center, testifying that these were my brothers and sisters. I felt an intense love for each one of them and a huge desire to tell them about Heavenly Father. My fear disappeared completely and I was anxious to talk to as many of them as I could. I understood in an instant, that truth that I had always known, but had not yet made mine: We are children of our Heavenly Father, which makes us brothers and sisters.

Since that time I've had other experiences. These have mostly come when I've been searching for specific truths and have been

---

46 Teachings of the Presidents of The Church, Joseph Smith (2007) 132

guided to read specific scriptures or articles, or talk with specific people. I've *heard* those truths, and I've understood in my head … but I just haven't been able to grasp it and make it mine. It has taken immense work in the thinking department, and a consistent motivation to keep trying and not give up. And I tell you, hard-work-thinking pays off. Because hard-work-thinking is actually having "real intent,"[47] as Moroni instructs us. And it always involves prayer. I have been rewarded, bit by bit, to have an understanding of those truths that have previously been mysteries to me. We are promised in the scriptures that mysteries will be unfolded as we desire,[48] diligently seek,[49] open our ears, hearts and minds,[50] and consistently ask.[51] All of those steps require thinking. And thinking truly is hard work!

There are other things that can promote success with intentional thinking. Included in that list is temple worship. Where better than the place eternal truths are taught in their most complete and concise form to have our thinking enhanced and mysteries made known? And I believe that where our thoughts are as we participate in temple work determines whether we are "attending" the temple or "worshipping" in the temple. The same holds true for our church meetings as well as our scripture study and personal prayers. We can either be *worshipping* or we can just be going through the motions. At the beginning of this chapter we talked about President Joseph F. Smith whose pondering, reflecting, and wondering preceded the revelation now known as Doctrine and Covenants Section 138. This type of thinking - pondering, reflecting and wondering - describes *worship*. Thinking that is that deep and that intentional, requiring

---

[47] The Book of Mormon, Moroni 10:4

[48] The Book of Mormon, 1 Nephi 2:16

[49] The Book of Mormon, 1 Nephi 10:19

[50] The Book of Mormon, Mosiah 2:9

[51] The Doctrine and Covenants 42:61

the Spirit to be present, becomes sacred. It is sacred thinking that leads to understanding. And real understanding of *all truth* comes only through the Spirit.

Not knowing how long Adam and Eve were in the Garden of Eden before making the choice to partake of the fruit, I wonder about how they spent their time. Certainly, sacred thinking was a part of their activity. Because in order to have made the decision that they did, they had to have studied it out in their minds,[52] conversed about it, prayed about it, pondered on it, reflected on the things they had been taught directly from God, and without a doubt, they wondered at the majesty, the greatness, and the huge responsibility of their callings. It was this purposeful and intentional thinking that led to their inspired actions to partake of the fruit. Without that thinking, they would still be in the Garden, and the Plan of Happiness would be at a stand-still. I marvel at how vital proper, intentional thinking is! With Adam and Eve as our models, shouldn't we all put equal effort into our personal thinking? Shouldn't we carefully examine our situations, study our options out in our minds, talk about them, pray about them, personally ponder about them, and reflect on the information we've been given already through the Spirit? It is by so doing that we receive inspiration and personal revelation vital to our eternal growth. Why is this vital? Because we cannot access the Atonement without first having our hearts, our minds, and our actions in the right place. Adam and Eve made their thoughtful decision to leave their place of comfort and peace, knowing full well that life would get hard. But they also knew that those hardships would be the very situations that would allow them to progress. *And* they knew that the required progression could only come through the Savior because of His atoning sacrifice. It had to start with making the choice to leave comfort and enter

---

52 The Doctrine and Covenants 9:8

hardship. And that choice could only come through intentional, worshipful thinking! So when it comes right down to it, each one of us must - more than once in our lives - make the choice to leave our comfort zones and move into a place of hardship so that we, too, may access the Atonement. What it really boils down to is facing the truth that we are currently at a level of progression that we can understand. And it all starts with our thoughts.

CHAPTER 3
OF THE IMMEDIATE GOODNESS OF GOD

This is a pretty strong, clear statement. The people of Mosiah saw that God's actions in preserving the people of Alma were immediate. But the people of Alma may not have seen it that way ... or did they? They were not immediately released from bondage. They weren't even released from it after a day of praying ... and another day ... and another day. How then, could Mosiah's people, and possibly Alma's people, consider it immediate goodness?

Perspective is an interesting thing. We all know the story of the blind men who stand near an elephant. They are each invited to touch the elephant and tell what it is that they're touching. Because of their various perspectives, they each think it is something different. The one touching a leg says it's like a pillar; the one who is touching the tail says it's like a rope; the man who feels the tusk says it's like a solid pipe; the one touching the underbelly is so surprised at what everyone else is saying, and he says it's like a wall; the man who feels the ear says it's like a hand fan; and the one who feels the trunk says it's like a branch. How we look at things, our past experiences, our current state of mind, and our desire, all play a part in how we see things. The people in

Zarahemla, we've established, were led by a king who exemplified righteousness. Because of their perspective they were able to sympathize with the strangers who were fast becoming their friends. And they were able to look at the whole picture and see the greatness of a loving Father who brought these strangers into their land. To them, *immediate goodness* was not at all an exaggeration. They saw a group of people who were miraculously led away from danger, delivered from bondage, and still firm in their faith. They saw a group of people who were grateful to be in Zarahemla, who knew how to work hard, and who followed a righteous leader. They saw a group of people who, though terribly taxed, refused to give in to hatred, anger, or disbelief. They saw a group of people who were likely stronger for having endured their hardships than they were before being tested. Mosiah's people were able to look at the situation from a unique perspective. Their hearts ached for the pain their new friends had endured, and their hearts rejoiced at their deliverance. From their perspective, I can understand that this situation was proof to them of the *immediate goodness of God.*

When we can see our own situations, as well as others', from an eternal perspective, we are better able to have the joyful goodness of God revealed to us. I've been thinking a lot lately about the mysteries of God[53] - what they are, when they will be revealed, and how they will be revealed. I've come to understand that in my case, there are many things that are mysteries to me, but that other people fully understand. And I've thought that perhaps when I am able to view things from an eternal perspective, at those

---

[53] The Book of Mormon, Alma 37:11

moments, mysteries may be revealed to me. What we *see* is relative to what we *desire* to see. For example, we may see refugees entering our country, using our welfare system, taking our time and our jobs. Or we may see refugees, being delivered from bondage, staying firm in their faith, and grateful for the respite they are receiving. It's the same situation - the same refugees, the same city - everything is the same. It's our perspective that varies. When our perspective is in a good place, regardless of the situation we are in or we see others in, we will be able to recognize the *immediate goodness of God*. At that time, our faith will grow, our testimonies will increase, our desire to do good and be good will become more ingrained in us, and we will draw closer to Christ. Mosiah's people saw the *immediate goodness of God* because they had the right perspective.

What of Alma's people? Many had been beaten, all had been threatened, some had lost family members. Probably many were hungry and they were all exhausted. Did they recognize the *immediate goodness of God*? The answer is yes. Before they made it to the land of Zarahemla, when they were finally freed from the threat of death if caught praying, "... they poured out their thanks to God because he had been merciful unto them, and eased their burdens, and had delivered them out of bondage; for they were in bondage and none could deliver them except it were the Lord their God. And they gave thanks to God, yea, all their men and all their women and all their children that could speak lifted their voices in the praises of their God."[54] All of this after just one day's journey away from their bondage! Surely the people of Alma recognized the *immediate*

---

[54] The Book of Mormon, Mosiah 24:21-22

goodness of God even before they were delivered. In fact, we know that is true. During their extreme hardship, they were commanded to stop praying. "... but [they] did pour out their hearts to him; and he did know the thoughts of their hearts....and they did submit cheerfully and with patience to all the will of the Lord."[55] This makes me realize that their prayers didn't just consist of requests for deliverance. Their faith in the Lord and His timing is remarkable. So, when they arrived in the land of Zarahemla, were welcomed and cared for, and when King Mosiah made known their circumstances to his people, I'm sure that the people of Alma were as grateful and joyful and thankful as the people of Mosiah were. And I'm sure they, also, recognized the *immediate goodness of God!*

This makes me realize that the depth of our conversion is far more important than how long we've been believers. Alma's people were all recent converts. They followed him to the Waters of Mormon, heard him preach, felt the Spirit, believed, repented, and were baptized. Then only a short time later, they were trapped and in bondage to some very wicked people. And yet, even though they were new to gospel truth, they did not waiver. They were able to see God's hand in their lives - even when their prayers for deliverance were not answered right away.

We are all at differing stages of conversion regarding various parts of the Gospel. With some things we are just beginning to understand enough to have a testimony of their truths. Other aspects we *believe* are true because of our faith in the Lord and His prophets, but we haven't yet received

---

[55] The Book of Mormon, Mosiah 24:12, 14

confirmation through the Holy Ghost. And then there are other things that we don't even know that we don't know! Some of us have been converted to many aspects of eternal truths for a very long time, and some just recently. But what matters is that conversion is a fluid requirement. We must become converted over and over again in order to have the vision and the faith that the people of Alma and Mosiah had. If we are to recognize the *immediate goodness of God*, our hearts and minds must be in a place to recognize it. Because the truth is, it's always there to see! Whether we recognize it or not is up to us.

Isn't it interesting that, not just at their deliverance, but even while in bondage, the people of Alma were blessed with the ability to see God in their lives? And doesn't that give much hope for all of us? Whatever situation we may find ourselves in, we are never alone. Our Father is always a part of our lives, lifting us, encouraging us, allowing us to grow, supporting us, and loving us. Do we recognize His *immediate goodness*?

It is possible for us to train ourselves to see His *immediate goodness*. Since it's always there, the responsibility falls upon *us* to do the work to see it. We can start by examining how we feel. Daily introspection is a good thing. When we can slow our lives down enough to turn inward (without becoming self-absorbed) and examine what's going on, if we are seeking "with real intent"[56] to recognize His goodness in our lives, that gift will be granted. Why? Because *everything* that comes from Heavenly Father is true. And all

---

[56] The Book of Mormon, Moroni 10:4

truth is manifest to us by the power of the Holy Ghost.[57] And so if we are seeking to see the *immediate goodness of God* in our lives, we are seeking for truth. If we are honest in our search, it will be revealed to us through the Holy Ghost and we will know it as strongly as we can know any truth. In our daily examination of ourselves, it would be prudent to label how we feel. *Regardless of what circumstances I find myself in today, do I have a sense of peace? Am I still carrying many burdens, but they are more bearable than they were yesterday? Wait! What about that one problem I had ... I didn't even realize I'm not carrying that anymore. It's gone and I didn't recognize it until I focused on this search for inward truth! Do I carry elements of hope, even while in the midst of this trial? Have I been able to work out a plan in my mind to tackle tomorrow? Is there a sense of serenity even though things appear to be falling apart? Do I feel some joyful anticipation and don't know exactly why? Am I a little excited about what tomorrow may bring? Do I feel a sense of satisfaction, even if I don't know specifically why I'm satisfied? Have I been able to take that jumble of thoughts and organize it so I no longer feel scattered? Do I feel a little "lighter" tonight than I did this morning?* All of these feelings testify of the *immediate goodness of God* in our personal lives.

Beyond our feelings how, exactly, is His goodness manifest? Is it shown in ways other than our inward feelings? Absolutely! There are at least five ways His goodness is shown to us, including mortal assistance, inspiration, revelation, mercy and grace.

---

[57] The Book of Mormon, Moroni 10:5

Another phrase that stands out to me, when thinking of His *immediate goodness*, is the tender mercies of the Lord. Six months after Elder David A. Bednar was sustained as an apostle, he spoke in General Conference.[58] He told about his first experience speaking from that pulpit. Just before he spoke, the choir and congregation sang an intermediate hymn, *Redeemer of Israel*.[59] He said, "Now, the music for the various conference sessions had been determined many weeks before—and obviously long before my new call to serve. If, however, I had been invited to suggest an intermediate hymn for that particular session of the conference—a hymn that would have been both edifying and spiritually soothing for me and for the congregation before my first address in this Conference Center—I would have selected my favorite hymn, 'Redeemer of Israel' … Near the conclusion of the singing, to my mind came this verse from the Book of Mormon: 'But behold, I, Nephi, will show unto you that the tender mercies of the Lord are over all those whom he hath chosen, because of their faith, to make them mighty even unto the power of deliverance' (1 Ne. 1:20). My mind was drawn immediately to Nephi's phrase 'the tender mercies of the Lord,' and I knew in that very moment I was experiencing just such a tender mercy. A loving Savior was sending me a most personal and timely message of comfort and reassurance through a hymn selected weeks previously." After hearing this message from Elder Bednar I began to look at the tiny tender mercies in my own life more closely. The assistance I receive daily in mortality is remarkable! It is noticing them that sometimes eludes me. But as I've worked to take notice, then to acknowledge in

---

[58] LDS General Conference, April 2005, The Tender Mercies of the Lord, David A. Bednar
[59] LDS Hymnbook #6

both prayer and often writing in my journal, I've become aware that His *immediate goodness* and His tender mercies are abundant! To get you thinking about how you are divinely helped through your mortal journey I'll share a few of my experiences.

I had just returned from an extended visit with my parents. With my mother terminally ill, there was much that my siblings and I could do to help our father care for her. I had my next trip already planned that would take place about a month after my return from this trip. When I got home, there was a lot to be done. It was just after Christmas, and we're pretty heavy on the decorations in our home. So taking Christmas down was a priority. But hey, I had a month! So I planned to space things out - take down decorations, do my visiting teaching, renew my temple recommend, get some income-earning work done, and more. But I felt an urgency, even though I knew there was plenty of time. To top things off, I caught a cold. A bad one! *Well, at least I have a month*, I thought, *to get rid of the cold so I don't take it into Mom's and Dad's home.* Even with being sick, the To Do List in my mind kept nagging at me. I felt a need to push through and get things done. And so I did. Christmas got packed away, work got done, I even got my visiting teaching and temple recommend taken care of - all this in just a week. Within a couple of days I realized I was even feeling better - BAM! - cold gone! And then I got a phone call. I was needed in Texas right away. I changed my plane ticket and just ten days after getting home, I was on my way to my parents' home again. It was on that plane trip that this verse of scripture came to mind, reminding me that His *immediate goodness* is often manifest in mortal activities.

There are all kinds of tiny, seemingly unimportant things, that prove to me that Heavenly Father is aware. He is mindful of what is important to me, even if it has no eternal consequence. Those are some of the things that build my faith and help me to remember that I am a daughter of God. I am important. Several years ago, for her enjoyment and for ours, our mother bought each of us daughters a t-shirt that says "Mom Likes <u>Me</u> Best!" Whenever we would all get together, we'd make sure we had our shirts. We have a plethora of group pictures with us all in our t-shirts and Mom wearing her shirt that simply says, "Mom." One time when we were all together, my shirt came up missing. And yes, even as an adult, I looked to my sisters to see who had taken it. Of course everyone denied it. And I believed them. After all, sibling rivalry has diminished through the years. A few days went by, and still no sign of the shirt. I didn't actually pray over it, but I hoped and searched and asked. It had simply disappeared! One morning, I got up before the rest of the family, went downstairs to open blinds, and sitting right there on the fireplace hearth was my shirt. Even though they're all identical, mine has a tiny hole in it, so it's easily identifiable. This time I did pray over it. A prayer of gratitude. Partly for the shirt, but mostly for Heavenly Father's acknowledgment of my desire. He knew it meant something to me, and although it was not important in the eternal scheme of things, He was showing me that He is aware of me. I could share the same story dozens of times over, just changing it from a t-shirt to keys, or an envelope of money, or a piece of jewelry. It happens so often - when something that is relatively unimportant becomes lost - and as evidence of His *immediate goodness*, it is found. Usually the little miracles and tender mercies come shortly after a prayer, which I've delayed because of the smallness of the need, but which comes of desperation.

When I was a teenager, my younger sister and I were involved in church volleyball.[60] Because I'd had my license for over a year, my parents agreed to let me drive my sister and myself to the regional volleyball tournament one Friday night even though it was pretty far away. On our way home, due to a faulty gas gauge, we ran out of gas on the freeway. Our van coasted to a stop and we were stranded. This was before cell phones and so we were really on our own as to how to get assistance. We prayed, of course, but after being passed by three police cars over the course of about a half hour, we knew we couldn't wait for that kind of assistance. So after another prayer, we decided to walk toward the exit in hopes of finding a payphone to call home. It was late, and a very dark night. When we were just a quarter of a mile or so into our walk toward the exit, we heard traffic slowing. Of course we hoped it was a police car, but when we turned to look, fright overtook us as we saw it was two motorcyclists. We both followed our instincts and ran straight back to the van, hopped in, and locked it. It was really scary, and through tears we prayed more. Not long after finishing one of our prayers we looked out the window to see, on the other side of the freeway, our parents in their car. They had found us. The *immediate goodness of God* was clearly evident in that rescue.

When we take time to notice the little things in mortality that work for our good, we become aware of His tender mercies and *immediate goodness*.

---

[60] The New Era, February 2000, The Three Questions

Perhaps one of the strongest ways His *immediate goodness* is manifest is through inspiration and personal revelation that we receive. Because this is always accompanied by the power of the Holy Ghost, we are less likely to see these as coincidence and more likely to remember the strong feelings of testimony that accompany this form of manifestation of His *immediate goodness*. Elder Richard G. Scott explained the difference between inspiration and revelation.[61] "When it is crisp and clear and essential, it warrants the title of revelation. When it is a series of promptings we often have to guide us step by step to a worthy objective, for the purpose of this message, it is inspiration." Both inspiration and personal revelation come to us because of His love for us. Of course, there are prerequisites to receiving both inspiration and revelation. Elder Scott continued, "One must be ever mentally and physically clean and have purity of intent so that the Lord can inspire. One who is obedient to His commandments is trusted of the Lord. That individual has access to His inspiration to know what to do and, as needed, the divine power to do it. For spirituality to grow stronger and more available, it must be planted in a righteous environment. Haughtiness, pride, and conceit are like stony ground that will never produce spiritual fruit. Humility is a fertile soil where spirituality grows and produces the fruit of inspiration to know what to do. It gives access to divine power to accomplish what must be done. An individual motivated by a desire for praise or recognition will not qualify to be taught by the Spirit. An individual who is arrogant or who lets his or her emotions influence decisions will not be powerfully led by the Spirit." So when our hearts, our

---

[61] LDS General Conference, April 2012, How to Obtain Revelation and Inspiration for your Personal Life, Richard G. Scott

thoughts, and our actions are in the right place, we are prepared to receive inspiration and revelation - both evidence of His *immediate goodness*. When I consider the personal revelation I've received, and compare it with inspiration, there is quite a difference. For me, like Elder Scott suggests, inspiration feels a lot like guidance and direction. It's being prompted to act in specific ways. Inspiration I've received includes thinking to pray for a specific individual, or do an act of service. Often the inspiration is in regards to helping another person. Sometimes the inspiration I receive encourages me to take action for myself. I may feel inspired to respond to someone in a particular way in order to stay true to myself; or I may feel inspired to change my routine to better my physical situation. For those who desire it, inspiration occurs daily. When we make Christ the center of our lives and "always remember him,"[62] we can claim the assistance He stands ready to give us through inspiration.

Personal revelation feels more like the peeling back of layers of knowledge to reveal truths. It is an understanding of something that has always been true, but I just haven't noticed, or grasped it before. Personal revelation results in pure testimony that creates building blocks of understanding, leading us upward and preparing us to receive more personal revelation. For me, receiving personal revelation is much like a treasure hunt. And why shouldn't it be? After all, "where your treasure is, there will your heart be also."[63] Don't we want our hearts aligned with God's truths? Of course we do! So as we are each on our quest for truth, we can be sure that His *immediate goodness* will be shown to

---

[62] The Book of Mormon, Moroni 4:3
[63] The New Testament, Luke 12:34

us as truths are revealed bit by bit, building stepping stones up to the next treasure quest. And like physical treasure hunts, receiving personal revelation requires a lot of work. We don't just ask a question, then receive the answer. Think of the Official Declaration shared by the First Presidency in September 1978, extending priesthood and temple blessings to all worthy males of the Church. Before the Declaration was read in General Conference, President N. Eldon Tanner spoke and said, "President Kimball has asked that I advise the conference that after he had received this revelation, *which came to him after extended meditation and prayer* in the sacred rooms of the holy temple, he presented it to his counselors, who accepted it and approved it."[64] This revelation for all the world came through the Prophet after much work. If, then, the Lord requires work of a prophet to receive much-needed revelation for the world, doesn't it make sense that He requires work from us to receive our own personal revelation? As I ponder on that concept I'm certain that Heavenly Father doesn't require work because *He* needs us to work, but rather, *we* need to work in order to be humble and have our hearts, minds and souls open so we can receive it. My experience in receiving personal revelation is that it truly comes after much work, a strong desire, and faith that it actually *will* come. Half-hearted attempts to understand something may lead us to some clarity, but it will not result in actual revelation. Perseverance is a must. My experience also reminds me that the feelings that accompany personal revelation are so strong and so sweet and so good that I never want to stop learning in the Lord's way. Understanding through the Spirit is one of the sweetest gifts I've experienced. And that makes me praise God for His *immediate goodness*!

---

[64] The Doctrine and Covenants, Official Declaration 2 (italics added)

Isn't the ability to look back and see past manifestations of His goodness such a gift? Often, in the midst of anything that is difficult to navigate, hard to bear, or even just muddled, it's hard to recognize the Lord's hand in it all. At least, for me it is. And so I wonder: When Adam and Eve were cast out of the Garden of Eden, and the ground was cursed, did they recognize that as the *immediate goodness of God*? Or did they see it as punishment? We know that they continued to worship Heavenly Father, and to ask for His guidance.[65] And we know that when God talked to them after they had partaken of the fruit, He told them that the ground would be cursed "for thy sake."[66] Were they able to see the blessing in the curse? We also know that if they hadn't made the choice to fall, as they did, they would never have known true joy.[67] And that could only have come about from the hardship they would experience in mortality. As we look at Adam and Eve's situation, we can see that the *immediate goodness of God* was manifest in everything that took place. But can we see it in our own lives? Can we see it in our own hardships and what appear to be punishments and cursings? How often do we ask *Why me? Why now? Why this?* Wouldn't we be better off to look at our situation as the people of Alma looked at their bondage? If we can find within us the ability to praise God and recognize His hand and thank Him in all things,[68] our eyes will be opened to recognize His *immediate goodness*.

---

[65] The Pearl of Great Price, Moses 5:4

[66] The Pearl of Great Price, Moses 4:23

[67] The Book of Mormon, 2 Nephi 2:23

[68] The Doctrine and Covenants, 59:7, 21

We know that if we allow it, all things can be turned for our good.[69] That means that whatever happens to us because of other people's choices; and whatever mistakes we make or sins we commit; whatever hardships come to us simply because of mortality; and whatever difficulties consume us, it can all be consecrated for our good. Doesn't that change how you look at absolutely everything? Knowing that to be an eternal truth, I am more easily able to forgive myself, forgive others, look forward with joyful anticipation, and feel honest gratitude to Heavenly Father for everything in my life. It also gives me the ability to recognize the *immediate goodness of God*. Do you think that when we are able to see the *immediate goodness of God,* we are in better shape, spiritually, to progress? Do you think that allows us to feel peace, regardless of our surroundings? And does it help us to lift others as well? I testify that it does all of that. If we look, today and every day, for evidence of God's *immediate goodness* in our individual lives, we will be happier, we will feel true joy, we will be motivated to work harder, we will have more patience with others, and we will love more completely. If we become intentional about seeking out proof of His *immediate goodness*, soon recognizing it will become instinctual. We will find ourselves offering silent prayers of gratitude throughout the day. We will feel lighter. We will strive harder. And we will have peace.

---

[69] The New Testament, Romans 8:28

CHAPTER 4
AND HIS POWER

There is much to explore and to discuss in regards to the power of God! After all, it is through His power that "the worlds are and were created;"[70] through His power that we can be redeemed; and through His power that we even exist. Through the power of God miracles have been performed, mysteries unfolded, and ordinances received. Through His power all things are possible. No wonder the people of Zarahemla gave thanks! They were first-hand observers of relief from bondage, accomplished because of His power.

When we study God's power being made manifest, we'll find references to the seemingly small (spring follows winter) to the magnificent (we will all rise from the dead, our bodies and spirits reunited, and become immortal beings),[71] and everything in-between. In fact, "...all things denote there is a God; yea, even the earth, and all things that are upon the face of it, yea, and its motion, yea, and also all the planets

---

[70] Doctrine and Covenants 76:24
[71] The Book of Mormon, Alma 11:43-45

which move in their regular form do witness that there is a Supreme Creator."[72] Yes! All things are evidence of God's power. I think that's one reason that feeling gratitude and expressing gratitude are so important. When we do so, we become aware of the magnificence of Heavenly Father, of His love for each of us, and of His great power. When we forget to be grateful, in essence, we're not remembering Him. And remembering Him - which includes remembering His Son - is part of the covenants we've made and continue to renew each week.[73] So how important is it to study about and be aware of God's power? In my mind, it is very important.

The scriptures are filled with acknowledgement of the power of God. Frequently, the title, "Lord" is followed by the adjective "Omnipotent" as part of His title.[74] "Omnipotent" is universally accepted as meaning all-powerful. Additionally, many scriptures, without using the word omnipotent, describe our Father and His Son as having all power.[75] Why and how is He so powerful? The answer, in part, is because He is perfectly righteous. His perfect righteousness and perfect obedience to natural laws makes Him all-powerful. Knowing this, it is understandable that for anyone to access God's power, it can happen only with righteous intent, obedient actions, and pure thoughts. God's power is not something that can be bought or sold;[76] and it cannot be used in any way that is contrary to His will. If we have

---

[72] The Book of Mormon, Alma 30:44

[73] Doctrine and Covenants 20:77

[74] The New Testament, Revelation 19:6;The Book of Mormon, Mosiah 3:5, 17, 18; Mosiah 5:2, 15; Doctrine and Covenants 133:16

[75] The Old Testament, Genesis 18:14, Doctrine and Covenants 19:3

[76] The New Testament, Acts 8:18-20

desires to access His power, we must be willing to submit to His commandments and His will. This requires not only humility, but also great faith and sacrifice.

The power of God is clearly evident in the recounting, by Willard G. Smith, of the massacre at Haun's Mill.[77] Willard was just 11-years-old when mobsters, acting as militia, rode into the small Mormon settlement, intent on ridding their area of Mormons. With no warning, shots were randomly fired and the result was the killing of fifteen men and two boys, with fifteen more wounded. Two of the massacred were Willard's father and younger brother. When Willard entered the blacksmith shop and saw death all around him, he was surprised to see that his other brother, Alma, was alive. Alma had been shot in the hip and his entire joint was missing. Amanda Barnes Smith, Willard and Alma's mother, had faith and humility, and was willing to sacrifice whatever was necessary to call down the powers of heaven for the healing of her son. In Willard's words:

> *"Our tent had been looted, even the ticking cut and straw strewn about. Mother leveled the straw and covered it with some clothing and on this awful bed we placed Alma, cutting off his pants to determine the extent of his injury. After placing Alma on this improvised bed, my mother, Amanda Barnes Smith, a woman of dauntless courage and implicit faith in her Heavenly Father, found that the entire ball and socket of the left hip had been shot away leaving the bones about three or four inches apart. As soon as Alma was conscious, Mother asked him if he thought the Lord could make him another new hip, and he replied*

---

[77] Museum Treasures, Blessings Amidst Tragedy, March 2015, LDS.Org

that if she thought he could, then he, too, believed it could be done. Then she called her remaining three children around the bed, and they knelt and supplicated the Lord for faith and guidance. Mother dedicated Alma to the Lord, praying that he be restored and made well and strong, but if this were not possible, to take him in his innocence. This picture of my Mother's implicit faith in her Heavenly Father remained as a living testimony to her children through their lives. In her terrible sorrow and bereavement, her only help could come from divine guidance. By inspiration, her prayers were answered and she knew what to do. First she was directed to take the ashes from a fireplace and made a mild lye solution with which she bathed the gaping wound until it was as white as the breast of a chicken, with all the mangled flesh and bone gone. Then she prayed for further guidance and was prompted to take the roots from the slippery elm tree and made poultices for application. She asked me if I had seen any elm trees, and I replied that there were some on the banks of the stream feeding the millpond. By this time, dark had descended upon this tragic scene, and when my Mother asked if I could take a shovel and get some of the roots, you can appreciate the terror which gripped my heart as an eleven-year old child. However, Mother assured me that the Lord would protect me and with a lighted torch of Shag-bark Hickory, I began my search. Women and children were lamenting loss of husbands, fathers, and children; dogs were howling, and the cattle smelling fresh blood were bellowing, and no one could know how many mobocrats lurked in the menacing shadows. It required all the courage I could summon to take the shovel, and with the aid of a dim torch, follow the stream and secure the roots from which Mother made a soothing poultice. The story of the miraculous healing of Alma's hip has been related many times, but few realize the constant terror of the stricken family, unable to leave the State as Alma could not be moved because of his injured hip; yet they were repeatedly warned that if they did not leave, they would be killed. They were forbidden to call the family together for prayers or even to pray vocally alone. This Godless silence, Mother said, she could not stand, so one day, she went down into a corn field and crawled into a shock of the corn which had been cut. After carefully ascertaining that no one was within hearing distance, she said she "Prayed till her soul felt satisfied." As she left the shock of corn, although there was no one in sight, she plainly heard a voice repeating these words:

> *'That soul who on Jesus hath leaned for repose I cannot— I will not desert to it foes. That soul, 'though all hell should endeavor to shake, I'll never, no never, no never forsake.'*[78]

"From that moment Mother said she had no further fear of the mob, and she inspired us children with faith that if we conscientiously did right, the Lord would shelter us from harm. Although Alma lay in the same position for five weeks while the wound was healing, strength seemed to come to the limb suddenly. One day, when Mother was carrying a bucket of water from the spring, she was alarmed to hear the children

---

[78] Hymns of The Church of Jesus Christ of Latter-day Saints, #85, How Firm a Foundation

screaming in the house. She rushed through the door to see them all running about the room with Alma in lead, crying "I'm well, Ma, I'm well!" Something had grown in to take the place of the missing ball and socket, and he was able to use the limb with no inconvenience. Although it was necessary in later years to pad the side of his trousers, he never suffered any pain or discomfort, although he filled a mission in the Sandwich Islands where he did a great deal of walking. As soon as Alma was well enough that we could plan to leave Missouri, great difficulties presented themselves, one being that our horses had been confiscated by the mob. Finally, I went with Mother to Captain Comstock, leader of the mob, and she demanded the horses, one of which was in the field. He said we might have the animal by paying $5.00 for its feed bill. This Mother could not do as all her money had been stolen by the mob. I admired her courage when she walked out into the field and tying her apron around the horse's neck, led it home with no further objections."[79]

Amanda Barnes Smith is a marvelous example of living so as to be prepared to access God's power.

Alma the Younger and the sons of Mosiah are also great examples of being endowed with the power of God. You'll remember that these young men begged for the opportunity to share the gospel with the Lamanites. King Mosiah took this request to God, and returned with an answer to the young men that they may go. For 14 years they preached.

---

[79] Museum Treasures, Blessings Amidst Tragedy, March 2015, LDS.Org

They endured hardship beyond what most of us will experience. Their righteousness, their integrity, their humility, and their obedience allowed them be filled with God's power. I love the example of one of these young men, Ammon.[80] Upon entering the land of Ishmael, knowing that the Lamanites would bind him and take him to the king, he was confident and prepared to do whatever it would take to share the truth with the Lamanites. Sure enough, Ammon was bound and taken before King Lamoni who questioned him. Ammon's honesty and humility were appealing to King Lamoni, who offered Ammon his daughter for a wife. Ammon politely refused and asked, instead, if he might be one of the king's servants. His wish was granted. As Ammon joined a group of servants tasked with watering the flocks, his heart was happy when he saw that he would be able to truly make a difference in the lives of King Lamoni's people. The servants became so frightened when the flocks were scattered by some rough guys, that they even began to weep.[81] Why so scared? When the flocks had been scattered other times, the servants charged with watering those flocks were put to death. They knew what was in store for them. But Ammon was actually pleased, "... for, said he, I will show forth my power unto these my fellow-servants, or the power which is in me, in restoring these flocks unto the king, that I may win the hearts of these my fellow-servants, that I may lead them to believe in my words."[82] And that is exactly what happened. Ammon encouraged the other servants and together they gathered the flocks and placed them in such a way that they would be protected. Then when the hoodlums came to scatter the flocks again,

---

[80] The Book of Mormon, Alma 17-20
[81] The Book of Mormon, Alma 17:28-29
[82] The Book of Mormon, Alma 17:29

Ammon took care of that problem. With a slingshot he killed some, those who got close enough to lift a sword against Ammon lost an arm, and the leader was actually killed by Ammon's sword. Ammon's fellow-servants were "astonished at his power."[83] Ammon was infused with the power of God which gave him both spiritual strength and physical strength. This experience opened the door for Ammon to share the Gospel with King Lamoni. When all of the servants returned from watering the flocks, they brought with them the arms that Ammon chopped off as proof of the experience they would share with the king. When the king heard this astonishing news, he was awestruck. He believed that Ammon must be the Great Spirit. Ammon was brought before King Lamoni, and through the gift of the Spirit he was able to discern the king's astonishment. As Ammon began to share the gospel with the king and those servants who were in the room, he made it clear that he was not God, but was a servant of God. "I am a man ... I am called by his Holy Spirit to teach these things unto this people ...And a portion of that Spirit dwelleth in me, which giveth me knowledge, and also *power* according to my faith and desires which are in God."[84] Because Ammon was righteous, obedient, and humble, he was granted God's power. And it was through His power that King Lamoni and thousands more came to know God and the beautiful Plan of Happiness.

How do *we* draw on the power of God? Essentially, we do just as Ammon and Amanda Barnes Smith did. We live, acting in righteousness to that progressive degree which we currently understand, having faith, and being humble. If we

---

[83] The Book of Mormon, Alma 17:36

[84] The Book of Mormon, Alma 18:34-35

are true to what we know, we can feel confident asking for, and drawing on God's power. We can take to heart the Lord's counsel to Oliver Cowdery, "Do this thing which I have commanded you, and you shall prosper. Be faithful, and yield to no temptation."[85] His commandments are given to us for *our* benefit. Heavenly Father wants us to be able to draw on His power. And that can happen only as we are obedient, pure in heart, and follow specific commandments. Righteousness qualifies us to have access to His power.

What else qualifies us to access His power? In January 2002, President Gordon B. Hinckley spoke to the children of the Church in the Friend Magazine. He said, "You are a child of God. You have His power within you to sustain you. You have the right to call upon God to protect you."[86] By virtue of our divinity, we have His power available to us. Remembering who we are, and *whose*[87] we are, gives us the confidence needed to draw on His power.

We know that it is through the Holy Ghost that we are taught God's truths. It is the power of the Holy Ghost that testifies, protects, directs, comforts, and instructs. The power of the Holy Ghost is God's power made manifest. If we are wanting to have access to God's power, we would be wise to remember Moroni's promise and practice his instructions regularly, to "...ask with a sincere heart, with real intent, having faith in Christ, [then] he will manifest the truth of it unto you, by the *power* of the Holy Ghost....And by the *power* of the Holy Ghost ye may know the truth of all

---

[85] Doctrine and Covenants 9:13

[86] The Friend Magazine, January 2002, Come Listen to a Prophet's Voice: God's Power Within You, Gordon B. Hinckley

[87] BYU Speeches, June 1989, That We May Prepare to Do Our Part, Ardeth G. Kapp

things."[88] Moroni's next words are not as frequently quoted, but are significant as we consider God's power. "...Wherefore I would exhort you that ye deny not the *power* of God; for he worketh by *power*, according to the faith of the children of men..."[89] Faith is required if we desire the manifestation of God's power in our lives. Faith in what? It is faith in the Lord, Jesus Christ that must be our core. The rays that emanate from our core faith in Christ include obedience, desire, gratitude, work, service, prayer, and charity.

President Russell M. Nelson gave us added counsel: "If we will humbly present ourselves before the Lord and ask Him to teach us, He will show us how to increase our access to His power."[90] What we don't understand, God understands. He will teach us all truths through the power of the Holy Ghost. We just need to humbly and sincerely ask.

It is amazing what can be accomplished as we access God's power through the Holy Ghost. I love this experience of President Gordon B. Hinckley which was shared by Elder Spencer Condie.[91] It beautifully illustrates the physical manifestations of God's power through the Holy Ghost.

> "I have a friend who is an attorney in Los Angeles. A few years ago he had a secretary with a terrible addiction to tobacco. After twenty years of smoking she had a strong desire to quit, and one day she walked into my friend's office and said: 'I notice you

---

[88] The Book of Mormon, Moroni 10:4-5 (italics added)

[89] The Book of Mormon, Moroni 10:7 (italics added)

[90] LDS General Conference, April 2016, The Price of Priesthood Power, Russell M. Nelson

[91] BYU Devotional, December 2006, Claim Those Exceeding Great and Precious Promises, Elder Spencer J. Condie

don't smoke.' My friend responded, 'And I notice that you do.'

"Assuming that everyone had faced a smoking problem at one time or another, the secretary asked her employer: 'Is there anything you could recommend that would help me quit smoking?' My friend reached into his desk drawer and retrieved a book with a dark blue cover and golden lettering and handed it to his secretary with the directions: 'Read this, and then you'll quit smoking.' His secretary was effusive in her gratitude: 'Thank you,' she said with a note of desperation.

"The next morning, to my friend's surprise, his secretary stormed into his office obviously very agitated. 'You promised me that if I read that book I would quit smoking,' she began with a voice tinged in irritation. 'I stayed up half the night and read 170 pages, and there wasn't a single reference to smoking.' My friend replied simply, 'Continue reading the book.'

"The second morning his secretary was even more agitated than the day before. 'I have read 330 pages,' she proclaimed in a raised voice, 'and there has not been one single mention of cigarettes or tobacco.' My friend smiled and said, 'Read on.'

"The third morning she was fit to be tied. 'I have nearly completed the book,' she said. 'I have finished 500 pages, and there still has been no mention of tobacco or of smoking of any kind.' My friend benevolently prompted her to 'Finish the book.'

"The fourth morning was different from the previous three mornings. She arrived quietly and somewhat subdued. She knocked gently on his office door and asked her boss if he might have a few minutes to talk. 'Of course,' he replied. Rather haltingly she started to explain what had happened the prior evening. 'I had a very unusual experience last night, and I'm not sure if I can really explain what happened, but I need to speak to someone about it. I finished the book as you encouraged me to do. Toward the end of the book, in the last chapter, I encountered a promise that if I would read the book and pray about it, I would know whether it is true.

"'Well,' she continued, 'I had already lost three nights' sleep, so I thought I had nothing to lose by putting the promise to the test. I knelt down and began a simple prayer, and as I was on my knees a warm feeling started at the top of my head and proceeded throughout my body, and I felt as if I were being cleansed and purified. And this morning when I arose, for the first time in twenty years, I had completely lost a desire to smoke. Thank you, thank you, thank you.'

"President Hinckley concluded the story by saying, 'I heard this story from her own lips as she was seated across the dining room table from me in the home of the president of the stake in which she was serving in the Relief Society presidency.'"

The power of the Holy Ghost is God's power. And it is available to all of us as we exercise faith, practice obedience, and have sincere desire.

One cannot consider the power of God without pondering the priesthood on the Earth today. The priesthood is the authority to act in God's name. It is conferred upon worthy male members of the Church age 12 and older. What is the purpose of the priesthood? "Priesthood is the means whereby the Lord acts through men to save souls," said Elder Bednar in the Priesthood Session of General Conference.[92] President Spencer W. Kimball stated it this way: "The priesthood is the power and authority of God delegated to man on earth to act in all things pertaining to the salvation of men."[93] Yes, priesthood is power - God's power - when appropriately used. When I think of priesthood responsibility, it is almost overwhelming - the authority to act in God's name! "To bear means to support the weight of that which is held. It is a sacred trust to bear the priesthood, which is the mighty power and authority of God. Think of this: the priesthood conferred upon us is the very same power and authority through which God created this and numberless worlds, governs the heavens and the earth, and exalts His obedient children."[94] A weighty responsibility, indeed! But also a tender gift. It has been said many times that those who bear the priesthood cannot use it selfishly. It can only be used to bless another. I love our all-wise, all-loving Heavenly Father, who knew that in our fallen nature we would need the priesthood - not only the ability to access His power, but also a reminder to serve others!

---

[92] LDS General Conference, April 2012, The Powers of Heaven, David A. Bednar

[93] Ensign, June 1975, The Example of Abraham, Spencer W. Kimball

[94] LDS General Conference, April 2016, The Price of Priesthood Power, Russell M. Nelson

The scriptures and the living prophets have taught us much regarding the difference between priesthood authority and priesthood power. "We have done very well at distributing the authority of the priesthood. We have priesthood authority planted nearly everywhere. ... But distributing the authority of the priesthood has raced, I think, ahead of distributing the power of the priesthood."[95] What does this mean? It means that authority and power are not the same thing. Authority is bestowed, power is earned. Elder Bednar was eloquent with his explanation: "Priesthood holders ... need both authority and power - the necessary permission and the spiritual capacity to represent God in the work of salvation."[96] He further explained, "Ordinary men are given the authority of the priesthood. Worthiness and willingness—not experience, expertise, or education—are the qualifications for priesthood ordination." But what qualifies these men who have been ordained to the priesthood, to access priesthood *power*? Elder Bednar has the answer: "Power ... requires personal righteousness, faithfulness, obedience, and diligence. A boy or a man may receive priesthood authority by the laying on of hands but will have no priesthood power if he is disobedient, unworthy, or unwilling to serve." Appropriate use of priesthood authority results in great blessings - the blessings Heavenly Father desires for those who are recipients of priesthood service. "When priesthood authority is exercised properly, priesthood bearers do what He would do if He were present."[97] The Doctrine and Covenants teaches us, in detail, the qualifications for priesthood power and the way to exercise the priesthood. Section 121

---

[95] LDS General Conference, April 2010, The Power of the Priesthood, Boyd K. Packer

[96] LDS General Conference, April 2012, The Powers of Heaven, David A. Bednar

[97] LDS General Conference, April 2016, The Price of Priesthood Power, Russell M. Nelson

instructs us, both those who bear the priesthood, and those who call on priesthood power to fulfill callings and assignments. This means that both men and women can and should benefit from the instruction in Doctrine and Covenants, Section 121. "We are not accustomed to speaking of women having the authority of the priesthood in their Church callings, but what other authority can it be? When a woman—young or old—is set apart to preach the gospel as a full-time missionary, she is given priesthood authority to perform a priesthood function. The same is true when a woman is set apart to function as an officer or teacher in a Church organization under the direction of one who holds the keys of the priesthood. Whoever functions in an office or calling received from one who holds priesthood keys exercises priesthood authority in performing her or his assigned duties."[98] So, whether we're parenting, teaching a class, leading an organization, or serving in any way, Section 121 is a great source to understand how we can draw on the powers of heaven. We read, "... the rights of the priesthood are inseparably connected with the *powers* of heaven, and that the *powers* of heaven cannot be controlled nor handled only upon the principles of *righteousness*. That they may be conferred upon us, it is true; but when we undertake to cover our sins, or to gratify our pride, our vain ambition, or to exercise control or dominion or compulsion upon the souls of the children of men, in any degree of unrighteousness, behold, the heavens withdraw themselves; the Spirit of the Lord is grieved; and when it is withdrawn, Amen to the priesthood or the authority of that man... No *power* or influence can or ought to be maintained by virtue of the

---

[98] LDS General Conference, April 2014, The Keys and Authority of the Priesthood, Dallin H. Oaks

priesthood, only by persuasion, by long-suffering, by gentleness and meekness, and by love unfeigned; By kindness, and pure knowledge, which shall greatly enlarge the soul without hypocrisy, and without guile ..."[99] Yes, priesthood authority is bestowed. Priesthood *power* is earned by righteous living. And priesthood *power* is the *power* of God.

As we live righteously, our confidence grows and we are then able to access God's power for our own profit and learning. Isn't it interesting how everything good comes from righteousness? Is it any wonder that Heavenly Father has given us so many commandments? He wants us to draw on His power! He wants us to be endowed with knowledge and direction. And He knows that can only happen for those who are pure. Therefore, the commandments are a gift to us - they are our outline to become pure and to be righteous so that we may progress. Let's continue with Doctrine and Covenants Section 121 to more clearly understand this truth. "Let thy bowels also be full of charity towards all men, and to the household of faith, and let virtue garnish thy thoughts unceasingly; then shall thy confidence wax strong in the presence of God; and the doctrine of the priesthood shall distil upon thy soul as the dews from heaven. The Holy Ghost shall be thy constant companion, and thy scepter an unchanging scepter of righteousness and truth; and thy dominion shall be an everlasting dominion, and without compulsory means it shall flow unto thee forever and ever."[100] As we live righteously, our thoughts, our hearts, and our actions being consistent with the Savior's teachings, we will not only be blessed with God's power (the ability to

---

[99] Doctrine and Covenants 121:36-42 (italics added)
[100] Doctrine and Covenants 121:45-46

access priesthood power) but we will also be blessed with increased knowledge that will ensure our progression. Why is increasing our knowledge through God's power important? Why do we care about understanding the "doctrine of the priesthood"? And anyway, what exactly *is* the doctrine of the priesthood? Without writing an entire book on these two verses, let's explore just a little. We know that the priesthood is eternal.[101] Because everything ever created, ordinances bestowed, and things yet to be revealed are all performed through the *power* of the priesthood, could it be that the doctrine of the priesthood is the knowledge required for eternal progression? Elder Bruce R. McConkie taught, "The Creation, the Fall, and the Atonement... are inseparably woven together to form one plan of salvation. No one of them stands alone; each of them ties into the other two; and without a knowledge of all of them, it is not possible to know the truth about any one of them ... The Lord expects us to believe and understand the true doctrine of the Creation ... Indeed, as we shall see, an understanding of the doctrine of creation is essential to salvation. Unless and until we gain a true view of the creation of all things we cannot hope to gain that fulness of eternal reward which otherwise would be ours."[102] So is it essential to, through the power of the Holy Ghost, have the "doctrine of the priesthood ... distil upon [our souls] as the dews from heaven," by living righteously? Absolutely. And isn't the poetic description pefectly beautiful? Those doctrines won't come crashing down on us like a downpour of rain. Instead, they will distil upon our souls. Like dew. Just lightly, gently, bit-by-bit, consistently, freshly, and purely. And by distilling, those drops of knowledge will come to us in ways that we will understand

---

[101] The Book of Mormon, Alma 13:7

[102] Ensign Magazine, June 1982, Christ and the Creation, Bruce R. McConkie

and be able to mentally digest. The knowledge will be taught to us through the power of the Holy Ghost. Our understanding will be firm, and we will be prepared to learn more.

As we consider the power of the priesthood and its manifestation, many of us will be drawn to experiences we've had. Often those experiences include miracles. Miracles of healing, safety, and spiritual growth come about when we draw on the powers of God through priesthood blessings. Brigham Young wrote in his journal about witnessing a day of healing. That day is recounted by Debbie Birch in an article titled, *A Day of God's Power.*

> *"July 1839.—President Joseph Smith had taken the sick into his house and door-yard until his house was like an hospital and he had attended upon them until he was taken sick himself and confined to his bed several days.*

> *"July 22, 1839.—Joseph arose from his bed of sickness, and the power of God rested upon him. He commenced in his own house and door-yard, commanding the sick, in the name of Jesus Christ, to arise and be made whole, and they were healed according to his word. He then continued to travel from house to house from tent to tent upon the bank of the river, healing the sick as he went until he arrived at the upper stonehouse, where he crossed the river in a boat, accompanied by several of the Quorum of the Twelve, and landed in Montrose.*

> *"He walked into the cabin where I was lying sick, and commanded me, in the name of Jesus Christ, to arise*

and be made whole. I arose and was healed, and followed him and the brethren of the Twelve into the house of Elijah Fordham, who was supposed to be dying, by his family and friends. Joseph stepped to his bedside, took him by the hand and commanded him, in the name of Jesus Christ, to arise and be made whole. His voice was as the voice of God. Brother Fordham instantly leaped from his bed, called for his clothing and followed us into the street.

"We then went into the house of Joseph B. Noble, who also lay very sick, and he was healed in the same manner; and when, by the power of God granted unto him, Joseph had healed all the sick, he recrossed the river and returned to his home. This was a day never to be forgotten."

Priesthood authority, when exercised righteously, yields God's power, and benefits all those willing to receive. Elder D. Todd Christofferson taught us that it is through priesthood ordinances that we make covenants which allow us access to God's power. "Our access to that power is through our covenants with Him. A covenant is an agreement between God and man, an accord whose terms are set by God. In these divine agreements, God binds Himself to sustain, sanctify, and exalt us in return for our commitment to serve Him and keep His commandments."[103] He further explains that in keeping the covenants we make, God is bound to keep His promises to us. It is those promises that infuse us with His power. And His power gives us the strength and

---

[103] LDS General Conference, April 2009, The Power of Covenants, D. Todd Christofferson

added blessings we need to continue our progression. "Our covenant commitment to Him permits our Heavenly Father to let His divine influence, 'the power of godliness' (D&C 84:20), flow into our lives," Elder Christofferson said.

Access to God's *power* is not limited by station in life, age, experience, career, or money. It is available to all who are humble seekers after righteousness. Just as Alma's people were recipients of His power during their bondage and as they were delivered, we all may have that same gift through our hardships and triumphs. Indeed, *His Power* is available to all.

CHAPTER 5
IN DELIVERING

Deliverance ... isn't that what the Gospel is all about? The Atonement delivers us physically and spiritually. In that sense, deliverance is an act that removes us from bonds and sets us free, in the truest meaning of the word. But in mortality does deliverance always mean that we are removed from whatever it is that binds us? Sometimes we are delivered in the sense of being relieved, but not removed. Think of Alma's people for that amount of time (we don't know how long it was) when they endured hardship and bondage. They prayed for release, but instead, their burdens were made light. And they were made strong. In that sense, they were delivered. Does that happen in our lives? Undoubtedly. We may ask for a change in circumstance, but instead be granted a change in ourselves. Instead of being removed from the situation, we may be taught how to best cope. The very thing we wanted removal from may be the thing that will help us progress. Our all-wise Heavenly Father delivers us in the ways He knows are best. In the case of Alma's people arriving in Zarahemla, they were literally delivered, or removed physically. But I suspect their deliverance went beyond the physical and into the spiritual. We know they were led by the Spirit of the Lord.[104] And we know they were delivered both from bondage and out of the hands of the Lamanites.[105] We'll discuss how those are different in following chapters. For now, let's talk about what deliverance means for us.

We use the term "deliver" to mean a variety of things. Some say, "When is her delivery date?" Other ask, "When will she deliver?" When talking about Mary, the mother of Jesus, Luke said, "... the days were accomplished that she should be delivered."[106] So we know that women are delivered. But so are babies! What else is delivered? Pizza. The mail. Good news. Verdicts. A punch. *Deliver* can mean giving something to an intended recipient; giving forth information; striking a person or thing. And it can mean setting something or someone free.

The delivery of women from childbirth, and the delivery of infants from the womb are great symbols of the deliverance that the Lord offers us. Being pregnant was not hard for me, as it is for some women. It may be because of my years of infertility, so my mindset was different; or it may be because my body and mind are just made that way. But pregnancy was a good time for me. Sure, I couldn't keep my breakfast down, and I swelled and had aches and pains. But there were physical benefits as well as hardships. The headaches that have plagued me throughout my life didn't exist during pregnancy; I enjoyed food in a way I hadn't before; and feeling movement of life inside of me was spectacular. But even with how much pregnancy agreed with me, those last

---

[104] The Book of Mormon, Mosiah 24:17
[105] The Book of Mormon, Mosiah 25:10
[106] The New Testament, Luke 2:6

few days were … not unbearable, but really, really hard. I wanted the baby out! Now! Something clicked inside my brain and all I could think about was delivery. "Bring on the pain!" was my motto. And then the pain began. Living in a part of the world where no medication was offered during childbirth, I experienced, a few times over, pain that is indescribable. It was during labor that I hoped for delivery, prayed earnestly for delivery, and even begged for delivery. It was different than the anticipation of delivery I had felt those few last days of pregnancy. There was an urgency that I had never before experienced. My situation, wherein the only escape from the intense and almost unbearable pain was delivery, drew me to the Savior in a way that no other experience could. What I had taken on for nine months as my mission, and what I was laboring for hours to do, all culminated in the required and exquisite *delivery* of a baby. Deliverance was the ultimate goal. Everything I had participated in, hoped for, and worked for, led to being delivered. As the baby was laid in my arms and with tears and inexpressible gratitude, I thought, *it was all worth it.* Given the chance, and knowing the outcome, would I do it again? Would I teeter on the brink of death, working toward and praying for deliverance? I would. Absolutely.

None of us remember what it was like to grow in our mother's womb, finally to be delivered into our next estate. But we do know that babies go from being completely surrounded by comfort, warmth, and protection to breathing dry air, and being exposed to bright lights, loud noise, and cold air. The shock must be incredible. Babies are delivered from a state of peace to a life of progression. They gradually grow out of their innocence as they gain knowledge and experience. And it all begins with *delivery* at birth. How is this symbolic of the delivery we receive through the Savior? Before gaining enough knowledge to make specific covenants like baptism and our temple covenants, we are in a state of relative innocence. Innocence carries with it a certain type of peace. Much like being in our mother's womb, we are growing, but only so far. *We must be delivered to move forward in our progression.* Baptism is often referred to as rebirth. Think of Christ teaching Nicodemus that he must be born again.[107] Birth, or delivery, is required for progression. When Christ was talking to Nicodemus, He continued with teaching Him just what the essence of the gospel is: The Atonement.[108] Delivery from innocence to an opportunity to progress includes accessing the gifts of the Atonement in our lives to the degree of our current understanding. In this sense, deliverance is continual. And it seems to me that regular deliverance throughout mortality leads us to a state wherein we are prepared for deliverance from mortality to immortality, and then to exaltation. In a way, accepting His continual deliverance in this life is *practice* that prepares us for the judgment day.

I recently had an experience that made me question, *How long? This is exhausting, hard work, not fun ... how long must it go on?* In talking with a friend, I voiced that thought. She gave me my answer by asking me a question: "Do you think the Lord ever wondered *How long*?" Silenced, my mind flipped into fast gear. *It's not the right question. Am I working toward a goal? An outcome? Deliverance from one situation into a better one? "How long" is irrelevant. It will take however long it takes. My focus should be on my acceptance of my part in bringing about the hoped-for result.*

---

[107] The New Testament, John 3:1-7
[108] The New Testament, John 3:14-18

That's what Christ did in the Garden of Gethsemane. He kept going as long as He had to keep going. He worked through it. He did it willingly. If my heart is in the right place, I will forget about "how long" and focus on doing what is required. And when the time is right, I will be delivered.

During the most intense part of my labors, I became unaware of time. In order to work through the pain so my body could accomplish what it needed to, allowing me to be delivered, it took all of my focus. I had to mentally work through the labor in order to get prepared for delivery. I could not be sidetracked into a pity party. I couldn't have my focus distracted, even to thinking about the amount of time I was enduring. I was literally required to focus on the work my body was doing. And then when it was time for delivery, the joy was so intense and the relief was its own level of excellence and perfection.

Jennilyn Eckersley shared this experience:
I learned this lesson many years ago in college. In trying to decide what my major should be, I took a wide variety of classes. One of those was Recreational Management 123. Each Wednesday evening we would participate in a different sport: skeet shooting, sledding a mile-long course, snowshoeing, cross-country skiing, etc. But I learned so much about myself the day we went spelunking. We lowered ourselves via a ten-foot rope into this underground cave. The belly-crawling through mud to get to a more open space where we could stand, was a bit uncomfortable, but not horrible. Squeezing through spots that looked like a crescendo marking in music, with one side almost completely closed and the other being wider open, took some doing. I wasn't sure I could get through some of those spaces, but there were

classmates behind me, so I needed to keep moving. When we reached the center of the cave, our professor had us turn off our flashlights. "This," he said, "is what total darkness means. There is no ambient light. Your eyes can never 'get used to the dark' and you become able to see." He had us put our hands in front of our faces and bring them closer and closer until we could see them. I was surprised when my hand touched my nose. I literally didn't see it coming! Though all of that taught me much, the real lesson was yet to be learned.

As we neared the end of our adventure we reached a several-foot-wide crevice. I'd have to jump – and without a running start. I hesitated, and though I'd seen the classmates in front of me do it, I lacked the confidence to try. Those behind me encouraged me, and those ahead of me continued following the guide, getting further and further from me. Eventually I took a deep breath and jumped. I did it! I hurried to catch up. But there was one more challenge ahead. I didn't consider, when I climbed down that ten-foot rope, that to get out of the cave I'd have to climb back up it. In PE class I never was able to climb all the way to the top of the rope. Not once. And now here I was. I stood by that rope for what seemed like hours, looking up at my destination. What were my choices? I could give up and die in that cave, or I could try to climb that rope. I felt the impatience of those behind me as I continued to hesitate. Staying down here isn't really an option And there's not really room for people to go past me so they can get out. I think I'm going to have to climb that rope. *And guess what! I did it! I had never been able to climb a ten-foot rope before, but when put in a literal do-or-die situation, I reached within myself and found the strength to do it!*

To be sure, every muscle in my body ached for the next few days. And I don't have the desire to ever go spelunking again. Ever. But what an invaluable lesson that week's activity taught me! I can do whatever I'm required to do, with the Lord's help.

The Atonement of Christ offers us deliverance in two ways:

As our *Savior*, He delivers us from physical death. "The spirit and the body shall be reunited again in its perfect form; both limb and joint shall be restored to its proper frame, even as we now are at this time; and we shall be brought to stand before God ... Now, this restoration shall come to all, both old and young, both bond and free, both male and female, both the wicked and the righteous; and even there shall not so much as a hair of their heads be lost; but every thing shall be restored to its perfect frame, as it is now, or in the body ... I say unto you that this mortal body is raised to an immortal body, that is from death, even from the first death unto life, that they can die no more; their spirits uniting with their bodies, never to be divided; thus the whole becoming spiritual and immortal, that they can no more see corruption."[109] This physical deliverance gives us immortality as a free gift to all. Having been delivered from the bonds of death, we will continue to live, with our spirits and our bodies reunited. There is nothing required of us to access this deliverance. We are granted this gift simply because we made the choice to live in mortality. The gift of resurrection goes beyond the incomprehensible joy of being immortal. Indeed, it gives our mortal experience more purpose. Elder Dallin H. Oaks taught that our knowledge of His deliverance,

---

[109] The Book of Mormon Alma 11:43-45

known as resurrection, "affects how we look on the physical challenges of mortality ... gives us a powerful incentive to keep the commandments of God ... helps us live together in love in this life in anticipation of joyful reunions and associations in the next ...gives us the courage to face our own death ... helps us bear the mortal separations involved in the death of our loved ones. Every one of us has wept at a death, grieved through a funeral, or stood in pain at a graveside. I am surely one who has. We should all praise God for the assured resurrection that makes our mortal separations temporary and gives us the hope and strength to carry on."[110]

As our *Redeemer,* He delivers us from sin. "We are all accountable to Him for our lives, our choices, and our actions, even our thoughts," stated Elder D. Todd Christofferson. "Because He redeemed us from the Fall, our lives are in reality His."[111] We are redeemed from sin, *delivered* from sin, as we repent and willingly progress. This deliverance, although offered with some requirements, is the second gift of the Atonement. We are delivered from a spiritual death as we exercise our agency to make righteous choices and to repent. "And thus mercy can satisfy the demands of justice, and encircles them in the arms of safety, while he that exercises no faith unto repentance is exposed to the whole law of the demands of justice; therefore only unto him that has faith unto repentance is brought about the great and eternal plan of redemption."[112] Progression is a beautiful gift as well. It says to me that righteousness is

---

[110] LDS General Conference, April 2000, Resurrection, Dallin H. Oaks

[111] LDS General Conference, April 2014, The Resurrection of Jesus, D. Todd Christofferson

[112] The Book of Mormon, Alma 34:16

relative to the knowledge I currently have. So, rather than condemning myself and believing I am not worthy of redemption because I just learned that I haven't been living up to a certain truth, I am encouraged to implement that newly acquired knowledge and progress from where I am today. But it also means that I must work hard to live up to what I understand today. With revealed knowledge comes responsibility to repent and do better. "Through the infinite Atonement, God has provided a means whereby we can both overcome our sins and become completely clean again. This is made possible by the eternal law of mercy. Mercy satisfies the claims of justice through our repentance and the power of the Atonement. Without the power of the Atonement and our complete repentance, we are subject to the law of justice."[113] Understanding this gives hope. We can hope for deliverance from damnation - or a halt to our progression. Through our knowledge of His delivering us from spiritual death, we can hope for exaltation and true joy because of His mercy. But to be delivered, we must repent. "We access the Atonement through repentance. When we repent, the Lord allows us to put the mistakes of the past behind us."[114]

My sister was widowed suddenly as a young mother. I've learned a lot about patience, endurance and deliverance as I've watched her. Following are her words:

---

[113] LDS General Conference, April 2006, The Great Plan of Happiness, Earl C. Tingey

[114] LDS General Conference, April 2011, The Miracle of the Atonement, C. Scott Grow

Only a few days after my husband's passing someone said to me, "I've been wondering why this happened to you. I mean, why not someone else? And then I realized it was because you are strong enough to do this." Those words, though well-meaning, cut to the center of my heart. So I was widowed young because I'm strong enough to handle it? I'd rather have him back than to be strong, *I thought. I've been asked essentially the same thing in dozens of different ways by dozens of different people: "How can you go on to raise your young children when your husband was taken from you so abruptly?" And the answer is simple – what choice do I have? Of course, I could choose to wallow in self-pity and make life miserable for my children, as well as myself, or I could do everything possible to give my children a good life, in spite of my difficult circumstances. I have become stronger because it was necessary. I have done what needed to be done, with the assistance of my Heavenly Father, in order to raise my children in a manner that is pleasing to Him. My sure knowledge that I can be reunited with my husband in the eternities gives me the will to go on. With my eye on the prize, so to speak, I can not only endure but also thrive in any circumstance in which I find myself.*

With a desire to live eternally in Heavenly glory, we gain a sense of purpose to our mortal hardships. It's like preparing for the delivery of a child. We do the work, looking forward to delivery, knowing the great joy that delivery will bring. We have ups and downs throughout the pregnancy - just like the ups and downs of mortal life. Sometimes we're sick, and sometimes we feel great. Sometimes we cope with loss, with just the future of eternal life cheering us on. Sometimes we battle hardship in a variety of ways. But always, we can look forward to what awaits us. And just like labor which precedes delivery, sometimes mortality is almost unbearable. But as we focus on what must be done, we press forward knowing that in *delivery*, we will be gifted with life.

CHAPTER 6
ALMA AND HIS BRETHREN OUT OF THE HANDS OF THE LAMANITES

From the foreword we know that the people of Alma were newly converted to the gospel of Jesus Christ and were living righteously. They had already left their land and their homes to escape the murderous priests of King Noah. Together, the group was living in peace as they practiced what they were learning about truth and love. They had already been protected from harm and bondage when their prophet-leader, Alma, was warned to take the group further into the wilderness to avoid those who would destroy them. And so it had to come as somewhat of a shock to them when they learned the Lamanites were coming after them. But they were a praying people, filled with faith. So they did just that; they prayed in faith. But this time they weren't led to safety and freedom.

Their leaders, having surrendered to the Lamanites, made an agreement which they thought would keep the group safe. But the Lamanites reneged and the situation became worse rather than better. It must have been frightening, and for some, it had to be disheartening. We know some details about their situation while under the thumb of the Lamanites.

"... Amulon began to exercise authority over Alma and his brethren, and began to persecute him, and cause that his children should persecute their children ... he exercised authority over them, and put tasks upon them, and put task-masters over them. And it came to pass that so great were their afflictions that they began to cry mightily to God."[115] I'm certain that their prayers were heard and that they continued to hope for relief. But before it got better, it got worse again. "And Amulon commanded them that they should stop their cries; and he put guards over them to watch them, that whosoever should be found calling upon God should be put to death."[116] So the people stopped praying vocally. But so great was their conversion and their faith, that they continued to pray in secret.

Why do you suppose they were taken by the Lamanites? We know that God could have kept them safe - he had done it before.[117] Had they made bad choices that placed them in harm's way? Had they become sinful? Why did the Lord allow them to be placed in this dangerous situation? "Nevertheless the Lord seeth fit to chasten his people; yea, he trieth their patience and their faith ... For behold, I will show unto you that they were brought into bondage, and none could deliver them but the Lord their God ..."[118] The answer is this: *Sometimes we don't know why.* Sometimes we get to look back and see the wisdom in past hardship - sometimes we don't. In the case of the people of Alma, they had not brought this hardship upon themselves. They were living Gospel teachings and were progressing. They had not

---

[115] The Book of Mormon, Mosiah 24:8-10
[116] The Book of Mormon, Mosiah 24:11
[117] The Book of Mormon, Mosiah 23:1-5
[118] The Book of Mormon, Mosiah 24:21,21

forgotten the Lord. Perhaps Heavenly Father knew that they could handle all that the Lamanites demanded and forced upon them; perhaps He knew that it would make them stronger and actually aid in their progression. Perhaps that is why reference is made to the Lord chastising His people in the scriptural narrative of this experience. He simply allowed the Lamanites their agency. Because He can turn all things for our good, perhaps His plan was for increased patience and faith for the people of Alma. Perhaps their horrible experience would benefit others - maybe even strengthen the testimonies of others. We know that it actually *did* have a positive effect on Mosiah's people in Zarahemla. Maybe the answer to *why* is multifaceted. It is interesting that this many years later as I read about their experience I actually don't know all the reasons! So why do I often think that I should know all of the reasons bad things happen to me?

Humbling to me is the recorded conversation that Alma had with his son, Helaman, telling him of the importance the records are for their people. Alma is preparing Helaman to be the next keeper of the records. I imagine the father and son talking and Alma is explaining to Helaman how the records have done so much good for so many. And then he begins to suppose what good will come of the records in the future. But in this instance, he doesn't actually *know*. So he says, "Now these mysteries are not yet fully made known unto me; therefore I shall forbear."[119] He further testifies to his son that God knows the purposes for everything. Here was Alma, a prophet and a great leader, wondering about something and accepting the fact that he just doesn't know the answer. The fact that he doesn't know may mean that

---

[119] The Book of Mormon, Alma 37:11

he doesn't *need to* know. Instead, he chooses to "forbear" and move forward. A great lesson!

I am reminded of the man who was born blind in Jesus' time. John recorded the teaching that occurred when Jesus and his disciples walked past the beggar. "Master, who did sin, this man, or his parents, that he was born blind? Jesus answered, Neither hath this man sinned, nor his parents: but that the works of God should be made manifest in him."[120] Remember what happened after that? Jesus healed the blind man. He wasn't the only one affected by the healing. It created quite a stir and an inquisition took place. The man's parents were summoned to testify that he really *was* born blind. Eventually the man himself testified, even though he knew his testimony would result in expulsion. And then the really beautiful segment took place. The man became spiritually converted to the Savior. How many others were converted because this man was born blind and then healed? We don't know. But here I am, centuries later, strengthened by the recording of that experience. It has taught me that some things happen simply so that we may witness God's works.

Being placed in difficult situations and enduring well requires faith in God and humble submission to His will. No, He doesn't like to see us hurting. But He often allows hurtful things in our lives because He loves us and knows we can grow from them. Remember what He told the prophet, Joseph Smith, and thereby told all of us: "... all these things shall give thee experience, and shall be for thy good."[121] It may seem a trite statement, but it is good to remember that

---

[120] The New Testament, John 9:2-3
[121] Doctrine and Covenants 122:7

often bad things happen to good people. It is because of agency and mortality. All choices have consequences and just *living* in a fallen world means that bad things naturally occur. But isn't it heartening to know that **all** things can be for our good? It is empowering, really. We may not be able to control some of the things that come into our lives, but we may certainly control how we endure them. If we're going to have to deal with the situation anyway, wouldn't we want to learn and grow as much as possible from it?

For Alma's people, as they continued to pray in their hearts for relief and release, their prayers were answered. They were not immediately taken out of the situation. But "... the voice of the Lord came to them in their afflictions, saying: Lift up your heads and be of good comfort, for I know of the covenant which ye have made unto me; and I will covenant with my people and deliver them out of bondage. And I will also ease the burdens which are put upon your shoulders, that even you cannot feel them upon your backs, even while you are in bondage ... And now it came to pass that the burdens which were laid upon Alma and his brethren were made light; yea, the Lord did strengthen them that they could bear up their burdens with ease."[122] Their prayers were answered with comfort, with the promise that their difficult situation would not last forever, but that they would have increased strength. Additionally, the Lord promised to make their loads lighter, and He did. I wonder, when I'm in a difficult situation and requesting deliverance, do I hear and accept His promises and His assurances? If I'm not immediately remedied of the problem, do I recognize that I am being strengthened, or that my burden is being

---

[122] The Book of Mormon, Mosiah 24:13-15

lightened? Do I continue to do what is required of me even if I don't see exactly *how* or *when* the Lord will deliver me? And do I do as Alma's people did and "... submit cheerfully and with patience to all the will of the Lord"?[123]   Do I continue to exercise faith as I wait upon the Lord? Or am I quick to belittle myself and point an accusatory finger inward at my lack of faith because the miracle I want didn't happen yet? Can I see the hand of the Lord in my life even while in the midst of hardship? Alma's people did.

Eventually, (we don't know how long they were stuck with the Lamanites as their masters) they were delivered out of the hands of the Lamanites. They were physically freed. It was miraculous! It happened because of their patience and their great faith.[124] They had proven themselves. "And [the Lord] said unto Alma: Thou shalt go before this people, and I will go with thee and deliver this people out of bondage. Now it came to pass that Alma and his people in the night-time gathered their flocks together, and also of their grain; yea, even all the night-time were they gathering their flocks together. And in the morning the Lord caused a deep sleep to come upon the Lamanites, yea, and all their task-masters were in a profound sleep. And Alma and his people departed into the wilderness."[125]

I find it interesting that the Lord didn't just make the Lamanites disappear. He didn't just kill them all off. He didn't magically transport Alma's people to a new location. He told Alma to prepare, and that He would be with them as they escaped. I don't know if Alma and his people knew that

---

[123] The Book of Mormon, Mosiah 24:15
[124] The Book of Mormon, Mosiah 24:16
[125] The Book of Mormon, Mosiah 24:17-20

the Lord would cause the task-masters to fall asleep or not. It's quite possible that they only knew that they should prepare, but had no other information. They had faith. And they did the work required to leave. It was literally a sleepless night for them as they gathered all of their belongings. All the while, possibly wondering how the Lord would free them … but it didn't stop them from doing what was required. Their faith carried them forward. The people of Alma were delivered from the Lamanites *after* they had truly been patient, had continued in their covenants, and had exercised great faith. Not only that, but they had truly endured, and did so cheerfully.

If I hope for delivery from my hardships, I would do well to emulate the people of Alma. I'm grateful to have this record of the people of Alma to remind me that there is deliverance from hardship. But being delivered from our enemies, from difficult situations, and from hard things doesn't happen just to other people. I'm grateful to have kept occasional journals throughout my life and when I'm wondering how I'll get through a current trial, remembering my past experience is helpful. Experiences of people I'm close to also buoy me up. Their sharing of what they endured and *how* they endured strengthens me and gives me resolve to keep trying. I hope that with each new trial I am just a little bit more cheerful, exercise a little bit more faith, endure a little more gracefully, and grow a little more patient than the previous trial. The people of Alma were stellar people! I may not be at the spiritual point they were but rather than let it discourage me, I can choose to let it lead me.

Reality tells us, though, we are not all delivered out of the hands of our enemies; we are not all set free from every bondage; we are not all led to escape our hardships. What then? We remember that submitting to His will brings about peace and growth. We find the blessings even in the midst of hardship. We learn to live *through* it, patiently waiting on the Lord and doing all that He asks of us. Rather than asking *why,* we focus on what. *What* would the Lord have me do? *What* can I learn right at this very minute? *What* do I hope for? *What* is the Lord telling me in answer to my prayers?

Yes, sometimes bad things happen to good people. Sometimes I have situations that I think I might not be able to endure. Sometimes life is really, *really* unfair. But one way or another, eventually we will be delivered. It may be a physical deliverance from a hardship, or our deliverance may come in the form of increased strength and testimony. However and whenever it comes, we can be like the people of Alma whose faith never faltered, who continued in mighty prayer, and who submitted cheerfully, knowing that through our faith and diligence, Heavenly Father will at some point deliver us out of the hands of whatever holds us captive.

CHAPTER 7
AND OF BONDAGE

When I first began studying this verse of scripture I found it curious that the word "and" was placed here. So they were delivered in two ways:

      1. Out of the hands of their enemies

      2. Out of bondage

It's interesting to me that those are not one and the same. The more I studied the more I came to understand that physical delivery from a situation can be quite different than delivery from various forms of bondage. Bondage basically means being subject to someone or something other than yourself. It infers that your agency is taken away.

The people of Alma had been in danger of physical bondage before. At the time of their conversion, wicked King Noah had them pursued, but they were delivered. They also knew what it was like to be released from spiritual bondage. Before they were ever taken by the Lamanites, Alma taught them, "…ye have been oppressed by king Noah, and have been in bondage to him and his priests, and have been brought into iniquity by them; therefore ye were bound with the bands of iniquity. And now as ye have been delivered by the power of God out of these bonds; yea, even out of the hands of king Noah and his people, and also from the bonds of iniquity, even so I desire that ye should stand fast in this liberty wherewith ye have been made free."[126] So these people knew what bondage *and* what deliverance felt like.

Alma's people were clearly in bondage to the Lamanites. They were literally their slaves, required to perform all hard labor, being beaten, threatened with death, and more. They were clearly delivered from the bondage inflicted by their enemies. But it's likely that some, or all of them, may have required delivery from other bondage. And really, don't we all? Think of the ten lepers who, when Jesus approached, called out to Him and asked that He would have mercy on them. These were certainly men who believed in Jesus' miracles and hoped for deliverance. They knew He could heal them, if He would. And so they called upon Christ and they were delivered from their physical situation. All of them. As they followed the Lord's command to "Go shew yourselves unto the priests ... they were cleansed."[127] It was the single leper who returned to give thanks, who was delivered from spiritual bondage. "And one of them, when he saw that he was healed, turned back, and with a loud voice glorified God, and fell down on his face at his feet, giving him thanks ... And he said unto him, Arise, go thy way: thy faith hath made the whole."[128] How often have we sought physical deliverance, and been granted - and recognized! - relief from spiritual bondage?

Have you ever felt emotionally trapped? Maybe you've been stuck in a bad job with little or no potential for growth. Or maybe you've been in a bad relationship and you could see

---

[126] The Book of Mormon, Mosiah 23:12-13
[127] The New Testament, Luke 17:14
[128] The New Testament, Luke 17:15,16,19

no way out. Have you ever felt just plain stuck in life? You can't quite put your finger on the problem, but it's almost as if, in your frustration, you could rattle the prison doors which are holding you? Or maybe you've experienced the dark, heavy chains of willful sinning. You're told you can just stop it and be made whole, but to you, it feels as if you're truly chained and there is no escape. That kind of bondage kills hope and just seems to get more and more impenetrable. An attempt to escape seems futile and you might even wonder why you would *want* to escape.

Delivery from emotional and spiritual bondage can occur only with the help of the Savior. When we're told that Christ's Atonement covers *everything*, it's really true. He didn't suffer just for the sinner, but for those sinned against as well. He didn't atone just so He could succor us when grieving, but so He could release us from our fears and anger too. When appropriately accessed, His Atonement breaks all the chains that bind us.

Satan is a tricky bad-guy. Some of us live years and years in bondage, not even realizing it. We believe his lies including:
- You deserve this situation
- It's just who you are - you can't change
- There's nothing wrong with this
- It's not your fault - you were raised that way
- They need you - only you can fix them
- It's no big deal
- It'll all get worked out in the next life
- It's just a bad habit - you can stop anytime
- What you're doing isn't so bad
- No one cares anyway
- You can work on it later

- You can fix this alone – no need for the Savior
- This is too shameful to share with anyone

The lies are numberless. But even if we don't realize we're in bondage, if we look closely at ourselves we'll know that there is some dis-ease. We aren't quite comfortable with ourselves - something is out of whack. Let's talk about disease for a moment. I have some brothers who are etymology fans, and although I don't share their obsessions, I do find the origins and meanings of some words enlightening. Disease, for instance, comes from Old French. The word was *desaise* - the French *aise* translating to English *ease*, and of course the prefix *dis* means *lack of*. So, even when our bodies seem to be healthy, are we experiencing some emotional dis-ease? It's something to think about.

In speaking of Satan and his thriving in darkness, Nephi said, "...yea, and he leadeth them by the neck with a flaxen cord, until he bindeth them with his strong cords forever."[129] This is Satan's method to keep us unaware of our bondage and our need for continual use of the Atonement. His flaxen cords are so soft, almost imperceptible. If we aren't hyper-vigilant, he'll wrap them around us one by one until they become strong cords.

Looking from the outside, in - have you ever wondered how a kidnap victim with every opportunity to leave, chooses to stay? Or why a battered spouse doesn't leave? It seems so obvious to those on the outside, so clear how horrible that bondage is. It's inconceivable that anyone would choose to

---

[129] The Book of Mormon, 2 Nephi 26:22

stay in those situations. Yet that is exactly what we all do when we believe any of those lies Satan whispers to us. We become so comfortable in our situation that we can't see it for what it is: Bondage.

The LDS Addiction Recovery Program[130] offers help in recognizing the bondage we may be in. After all, what are addictions if they aren't bondage? When our will is taken from us, when we can't seem to control our actions or our thoughts, that is true bondage. We are slaves to the addiction - or the bad behavior. All of us can benefit from following the 12 steps outlined in the Addiction Recovery Program. Broken down into its simplest form, they are 12 steps to allow the Atonement to work in our lives. Any un-Christ-like attributes we are feeding and nourishing along are keeping us in bondage to some degree. We can do a lot of things on our own, but we need the Savior to completely free us from bondage.

Disney's Beauty and the Beast tells the story of bondage and deliverance so beautifully. How did the beast become a beast? He started out as a darling little prince. Sure, he was privileged, maybe even spoiled. But he was just a kid. As the prince grew, so did his sense of entitlement. With entitlement, he developed some pretty bad behaviors. He made himself all-important and forgot his purpose in life. The prince lived for quite some time in his sinful and self-indulgent state. He was unkind, uncaring, and downright mean. How did he get from being a darling, sweet little prince to a mean-spirited, self-absorbed snob? It was bit by bit, one flaxen cord after another. (I know - it's fictional. But

---

[130] AddictionRecovery.LDS.org

there's still a great lesson here.) The fact is, the prince has no idea he's so awful until he's cursed and placed in obvious bondage as the Beast. And it's interesting to note that for a long time, he doesn't even *try* to escape the bondage. He just stomps around and pouts about it. If anything, he dives deeper into himself and pushes all hope of freedom away. Also interesting is his blindness to the potential for freedom that Belle offers him. Instead of embracing her help, and *working hard* to make the changes required for freedom, he closes off from the opportunity even more. But Belle is quietly herself and able to see beyond his beastly appearance and behaviors. She sees the goodness in him and all at once, the Beast is able to forget himself and desires to please Belle. In the end, it is in losing himself, that he becomes his best self.

Pretty symbolic, right? Do we ever get so caught up in having to be right about everything that we don't even see the Savior offering us freedom? Are we sometimes so blinded that we can't feel His love?

The truth is that deliverance from bondage is available for all of us. The Savior isn't withholding it because we're not ready or because we're not good enough. He's offering it to all of us all of the time! We are the ones stopping ourselves from participating and accepting His gift. If we pray to have our minds and hearts opened to the changes which are required for us to be delivered, we will be taught. Although it might not be easy, it is simple. He stands ready to carry us through the hardship. Just as He went before Alma and his people as they were delivered, so He will do for us.

The Lord addresses all of us who are "called of God"[131] and gives us a very real promise. (Remember, *all* who have desires fit in that category!)[132] It's the same promise that Alma and His people received immediately before their deliverance from the Lamanites. The Lord tells us, "I will go before your face. I will be on your right hand and on your left, and my Spirit shall be in your hearts, and mine angels round about you, to bear you up."[133] It doesn't get better than that! I had an amazing experience while serving as a young missionary. It was the day after Christmas and I'd been on my mission just short of a year. I was being transferred to an area in Japan that hadn't previously had sisters. I was so excited! The elders helped me pick out the new apartment and to set up home because my new companion was coming straight from the Missionary Training Center. For several hours, I was without a companion as she was being welcomed at the mission home in Tokyo. I would be riding the train in later that day to join up with her and bring her back to our new apartment. The elders left after helping me move big things into the apartment. As I prepared for my companion to arrive by straightening out the newly acquired futons, putting away pots and pans, and connecting the portable water heater, I found myself completely alone for the first time in almost a year. It was really strange. Very soon the time arrived for me to journey to the mission home to pick up my companion. When I realized it was time to go, terror struck my heart. I had to leave the safe haven of my apartment … ALONE. I was not at all comfortable with this impending adventure. So I took a few deep breaths, knelt in prayer, then opened up my

---

[131] Doctrine and Covenants 84:86

[132] Doctrine and Covenants 4:3

[133] Doctrine and Covenants 84:88

scriptures and read for the few minutes I had before leaving. The page I turned to had a highlighted scripture: "I will go before your face, I will be on your right hand and on your left, and my Spirit shall be in your hearts, and mine angels round about you, to bear you up." Immediately a quiet peace settled over me. I knew I wasn't truly alone. Not only would the Savior go before me, but He had angels round about me. I put on my coat and shoes and headed out the door for the train station. I could almost physically feel the companionship of angels as I rode my bike the short distance. Then, although it was rush hour and the expected crowds were present, I was still at peace. Usually, if we were traveling at such a congested hour, the elders would travel with us and form a space for the sisters to stand, by extending their arms to the wall of the train so we wouldn't have to be pushed up against so many strangers. But I was traveling this rush hour without the elders. One never expects a seat at rush hour - we are lucky just to be squished onto the train with everyone else. But this day, as I stumbled forward with the crowd to get on the train, right at the door I entered was a vacant bench! I looked around to see if someone needier than I would like to sit - but no one else seemed to notice the empty seats. I sat down on the bench - with open seats on each side of me as well as space in front of me where no one crowded in. In awe, I watched as passengers were pushed onto the train and the doors slowly squeezed shut. And as I watched hundreds of people endure the crowded ride, I wondered why no one took the seats beside me, and why no one crowded into the space directly in front of me. Then the scripture I read before I left the apartment came back into my mind: "I will be on your right hand and your left ... and mine angels round about you." My prayer had been answered. I wasn't traveling alone. No one sat by me or stood in front of me because those places were already taken. They were filled with angels.

It doesn't matter the particulars of the situations we find ourselves in - He paves the way and makes it doable. We just need to follow Him. He will deliver us from every burden if we will just accept Him.

CHAPTER 8
THEY DID RAISE THEIR VOICES IN THANKS TO GOD

These words create such a beautiful image - "they did raise their voices and give thanks to God." How intense, and how sweet. Mosiah's people were so overcome with gratitude and emotion that they immediately prayed out loud. I love that.

The people of Alma, the recipients of God's deliverance, likely joined in the vocal prayers being offered by Mosiah's people. Alma's people had much to be grateful for in addition to their deliverance! They were not only released from their trials and hardships, but afterwards were received so graciously and with such a strong welcome that it must have made their hearts swell. This wasn't the first time Alma's people gave thanks. We know that they gave thanks regularly during their time of bondage - most of the time, silently. I imagine that when Alma's people were with the people in Zarahemla who expressed their heartfelt feelings to God openly, it caused Alma's people to feel a freedom that ignited their whole beings. These were a people who were naturally vocal about their joy. In fact, when they were being taught the gospel near the Waters of

Mormon and learned about the covenant of baptism, they actually, "clapped their hands for joy, and exclaimed: This is the desire of our hearts."[134]   Then, partway through their escape toward Zarahemla, "they gave thanks to God, yea, all their men and all their women and all their children that could speak lifted their voices in the praises of their God."[135] So I'm sure they felt an immediate kinship with the people of Zarahemla, united in their love for God.

Years after this recorded experience, Alma's son, also named Alma, dedicated his life to teaching the gospel. He and his missionary companion, Amulek, had intense trials as well as great success. Some of the wonderful teachings we have today are from Alma and Amulek's preachings. Among those are some very direct instructions about prayer. "Cry unto him when ye are in your fields, yea, over all your flocks. Cry unto him in your houses, yea, over all your household, both morning, mid-day, and evening. Yea, cry unto him against the power of your enemies. Yea, cry unto him against the devil, who is an enemy to all righteousness. Cry unto him over the crops of your fields, that ye may prosper in them. Cry over the flocks of your fields, that they may increase. But this is not all; ye must pour out your souls in your closets, and your secret places, and in your wilderness. Yea, and when you do not cry unto the Lord, let your hearts be full, drawn out in prayer unto him continually for your welfare, and also for the welfare of those who are around you."[136]

---

[134] The Book of Mormon, Mosiah 18:11

[135] The Book of Mormon, Mosiah 24:22

[136] The Book of Mormon, Alma 34:20-27

Not long after Amulek taught about prayer, Alma instructed his son, Helaman: "Counsel with the Lord in all thy doings, and he will direct thee for good; yea, when thou liest down at night lie down unto the Lord, that he may watch over you in your sleep; and when thou risest in the morning let thy heart be full of thanks unto God; and if ye do these things, ye shall be lifted up at the last day."[137] The message is clear: Pray over everything all the time. Why? Is it because God needs us to let him know what's going on? Of course not. It's because *we need to pray*. Alma's people understood this. They were a praying people even when they were ordered to stop - they continued in silent prayer. Consider the carefully chosen words in the hymn, Prayer Is The Soul's Sincere Desire.[138]

> *Prayer is the soul's sincere desire,*
> *Uttered or unexpressed,*
> *The motion of a hidden fire*
> *That trembles in the breast.*

> *Prayer is the burden of a sigh,*
> *The falling of tear,*
> *The upward glancing of an eye*
> *When none but God is near.*

> *Prayer is the simplest form of speech*
> *That infant lips can try;*
> *Prayer, the sublimest strains that reach*
> *The Majesty on high.*

---

[137] The Book of Mormon, Alma 37:37
[138] LDS Hymnbook #145

Prayer is the Christian's vital breath,
The Christian's native air,
His watchword at the gates of death;
He enters heaven with prayer.

Prayer is the contrite sinner's voice,
Returning from his ways,
While angels in their songs rejoice
And cry, "Behold, he prays!"

The Saints in prayer appear as one
In word and deed and mind,
While with the Father and the Son
Their fellowship they find.

Nor prayer is made on earth alone:
The Holy Spirit pleads,
And Jesus at the Father's throne
For sinners intercedes.

O thou by whom we come to God,
The Life, the Truth, the Way!
The path of prayer thyself hast trod;
Lord, teach us how to pray.

What is it about prayer that makes it so vital to our well-being? Part of that answer includes humility. When we make prayer a part of who we are, we acknowledge our reliance on Heavenly Father. It is this humility that allows us to access His power. Progression is minimal without Heavenly Father's assistance. It seems ironic, but the truth is that we are stunted when we don't recognize our own nothingness. Our inherent divinity propels us to progress exponentially when we are truly humble. Prayer helps us become and remain humble.

We gain a testimony of prayer when we pray over everything. Offering prayers of gratitude and prayers of request frequently helps us become praying people. Before we know it, we pray constantly; prayer becomes our go-to action. Elder J. Devn Cornish shared a simple experience that illustrates the gift of becoming a person who prays over everything.

> *"When I was a young resident physician at Boston Children's Hospital, I worked long hours and traveled between the hospital and our home in Watertown, Massachusetts, mostly by bicycle since my wife and young family needed our car. One evening I was riding home after a long period in the hospital, feeling tired and hungry and at least a bit discouraged. I knew I needed to give my wife and four small children not only my time and energy when I got home but also a cheery attitude. I was, frankly, finding it hard to just keep pedaling.*
>
> *"My route would take me past a fried chicken shop, and I felt like I would be a lot less hungry and tired if I could pause for a piece of chicken on my way home. I knew they were running a sale on thighs or drumsticks for 29 cents each, but when I checked my wallet, all I had was one nickel. As I rode along, I told the Lord my situation and asked if, in His mercy, He could let me find a quarter on the side of the road. I told Him that I didn't need this as a sign but that I would be really grateful if He felt to grant me this kind blessing.*

"I began watching the ground more intently but saw nothing. Trying to maintain a faith-filled but submissive attitude as I rode, I approached the store. Then, almost exactly across the street from the chicken place, I saw a quarter on the ground. With gratitude and relief, I picked it up, bought the chicken, savored every morsel, and rode happily home."[139]

Mosiah's people, upon learning of the miraculous deliverance of Alma's people, *raised their voices* in prayer. They were together, not individually secluded, and yet they prayed out loud. Can you imagine the scene? The only experience I know about that comes close to this word picture happened several years ago. Our three youngest children were all the right age to participate in the Church's youth program, Trek. This happens every four years in the place of that year's Youth Conference and in place of camp for some wards. Trek is an experience for all youth, ages 12-18 and lasts a few days. The experience allows the youth to learn something of what the Mormon Pioneers experienced in their westward trek. They eat simply, pull handcarts, and gather around campfires at night. It gives them an appreciation for those who have gone before. On the last day of this trek that our children participated in, one of their leaders collapsed and died. It was sudden and shocking. He was a well-loved leader and everyone was stunned. The youth responded with tears and comforting each other, but mostly praying. In small groups of two or three they would kneel and offer vocal prayers. Many stood

---

[139] LDS General Conference, October 2011, The Privilege of Prayer, J. Devn Cornish

alone and prayed out loud. In the beautiful outdoors these kids, who had grown close to each other and to their leaders in just a few short days, had also grown closer to Heavenly Father. Their first reaction when their leader collapsed was to *raise their voices in prayer*. Just like the people of Alma and the people of Mosiah. Is that the way we are?

For those who feel awkward praying vocally, the remedy is to do it. Try first, alone in your car or in your backyard. Seclude yourself and *raise your voice in prayer*. The experience will be remarkable. Praying vocally brings a peace all its own. When we really internalize the truth that we are praying to our Father, our perfect Father who loves us completely, the fear or awkwardness dissipates. "As soon as we learn the true relationship in which we stand toward God (namely, God is our Father, and we are his children), then at once prayer becomes natural and instinctive on our part. Many of the so-called difficulties about prayer arise from forgetting this relationship."[140] There is power in prayer, and vocal prayer has a special power all its own. As we remember the purpose of prayer, our prayers become more genuine and more complete. "Prayer is the act by which the will of the Father and the will of the child are brought into correspondence with each other. The object of prayer is not to change the will of God, but to secure for ourselves and for others blessings that God is already willing to grant, but that are made conditional on our asking for them. Blessings require some work or effort on our part before we can obtain them. Prayer is a form of work, and is an appointed means for obtaining the highest of all blessings."[141]

---

[140] LDS Bible Dictionary, Prayer
[141] LDS Bible Dictionary, Prayer

Like Alma's and Mosiah's people, do we regularly pray in thanksgiving? In order to express our gratitude through prayer, we first have to *feel* grateful. "And he who receiveth all things with thankfulness shall be made glorious; and the things of this earth shall be added unto him, even an hundred fold, yea, more."[142] Additionally, the Apostle Paul taught the Thessalonians, "In every thing give thanks: for this is the will of God in Christ Jesus concerning you."[143] Do you suppose that Alma's people were actually *grateful* and offering prayers of *thanksgiving* while they were still in bondage? If so, how could that be? Is it possible to be in the midst of hardship and still be grateful? It's easier for some people than for others. I love this example shared in the *Ensign* years ago:

> *"A young mother knelt beside her three-year-old and listened to his heartfelt bedtime prayer. As he gave thanks for his big brother, for snow, for clouds, and for pizza, she tried to remember the last time she had thanked the Lord for such things. She realized that although she always thanked our Heavenly Father for things such as health, family, and the gospel, she had forgotten to remember the ordinary and simple blessings of her own life. When she began expressing gratitude daily for all these blessings, she saw the world with new eyes. She found that grief and hardship became easier to bear and that she was spiritually nourished."[144]*

It seems that even if it's tough to be grateful during hard times, when we make the effort to count our blessings and

---

[142] Doctrine and Covenants 78:19
[143] The New Testament, 1 Thessalonians 5:18
[144] Ensign Magazine, July 1995, More Gratitude Give Me

express our thanks to the Lord, the hard times become more bearable.

Alma's and Mosiah's people are great examples of expressing thanks. There are others whose experiences are equally inspiring. When Hannah, in the Old Testament, was finally blessed with a child after years of infertility, she expressed her heartfelt gratitude. "For this child I prayed; and the Lord hath given me my petition which I asked of him: Therefore also I have lent him to the Lord; as long as he liveth he shall be lent to the Lord."[145] The Jaredites, a group of people who lived during the time of the Tower of Babel, were led by God to the promised land. That meant that they spent nearly a year traveling across the ocean in barges. "And it came to pass that they were many times buried in the depths of the sea, because of the mountain waves which broke upon them, and also the great and terrible tempests which were caused by the fierceness of the wind."[146] Even while they were being tossed around in the ocean, they found reason to be grateful and to express that gratitude. "And they did sing praises unto the Lord; yea, the brother of Jared did sing praises unto the Lord, and he did thank and praise the Lord all the day long; and when the night came, they did not cease to praise the Lord."[147] The scriptures are replete with examples of individuals and groups who suffered hardship, yet felt and expressed gratitude.

It's inspiring that Mosiah's people appeared to be as intensely grateful as Alma's people were! Here, these new friends were the ones who had been greatly blessed by

---

[145] The Old Testament, 1 Samuel 1:27-28
[146] The Book of Mormon, Ether 6:6
[147] The Book of Mormon, Ether 6:9

being delivered, yet it was the welcoming committee who expressed prayerful gratitude. How are *we* when it comes to being mindful of others' blessings? Do we feel grateful enough to *raise our voices in prayer*? I'm reminded of my mother who regularly used her created phrase, "This is a fall-on-your-knees moment." When something absolutely wonderful happened to those she loved, she would not just offer a prayer of thanks, but would make sure she knelt for that prayer, and would invite whoever was with her to join in kneeling and praying. Her example continued to the end of her life. It wasn't too long before she passed away when her grandson was in an automobile accident. It was potentially serious, as the car was slammed across a few lanes of freeway and into the median strip. When the family got word that he would be fine, those in the house prepared for prayer. Mother's health was failing, but she insisted on kneeling. It was her last kneeling prayer, and it took more than one person to get her up off her knees when the prayer was completed. Her example of truly feeling gratitude for another's blessing, and expressing that gratitude in prayer is worthy of emulation.

Our mother also taught her children – both explicitly and through her example - that a whispered prayer is as much *raising our voices in prayer to God* as is a prayer spoken through a microphone.

Raising our voices in prayer, or when that's not appropriate, offering prayers in our hearts, is an opportunity to truly commune with our Father. Prayer is a gift from Him to us - a gift that helps us keep in touch with reality as we remember our divinity as well as our dependence on Him.

The deliverance of Alma's people from bondage is proof of the *immediate goodness of God.* What, in our lives, proves His goodness? As we follow Nephi's example to "liken all scriptures unto us, that it might be for our profit and learning,"[148] we will come to recognize God's goodness in our own lives. Additionally, we will be *delivered* from bondage, and will have opportunity to *raise our voices* in thanks to our all-loving Father.

---

[148] The Book of Mormon, 1 Nephi 19:23

I am in awe of
Ken Turner's
None Could Deliver Them
which gives life to this book as the cover.
A print of this painting hangs in my parents' home
and reminds me, each time I visit, of
Heavenly Father's interest in and direction in
each of our lives; and that
He will always deliver us.

A million thank-yous to
Jennilyn Eckersley,
Editor Extraordinaire.
Plus, you make me laugh.

DenaleeChapman.com

Other Books by Denalee Chapman

Conquered
YOLO: Lessons Learned from Eve & Esther
Just One Verse, Helaman 3:35

www.ingramcontent.com/pod-product-compliance
Lightning Source LLC
Chambersburg PA
CBHW060943040426
42445CB00011B/986